The
Awesome
Fatima
Consecrations

by Father Paul Trinchard

PUBLISHED BY:
META
P.O. Box 6012, Metairie, LA. 70009-6012

Prologue

The Fatima Message

What is FATIMA? By way of an introduction to this book, we will review a few of the pertinent highlights of the Fatima Message. In 1917, Our Lady made six monthly apparitions to three little children (ages ten, nine and seven) at Fatima in Portugal.

Our Lady built Her message on the **PERSONAL CONVIC-TION OF THE REALITIES OF SIN AND HELL.** She gave these little children an "overwhelming experience" of Hell.

Why did She do this? Hell is the only and ultimate **eternal evil.** Sin is the only and ultimate **temporal evil.** Hell is the consequence of sin.

THE PERSONAL CONVICTION OF THE REALITIES OF SIN AND HELL constitutes the foundation upon which the Fatima Message is built. Upon such a foundation, love of Jesus and Mary (Who are offended by SIN) and true love for oneself and others become real and compelling (and for the great saints among us as compelling as it was for the three seers of Fatima). **THIS PERSONAL CONVICTION OF THE REALITIES OF SIN AND HELL,** by God's grace, can lead one to make and live the awesome personal Fatima consecration -- a dedication of one's whole life to Jesus through Mary or to Mary and thus to Jesus.

"Offer up to God all the sufferings He desires to send you in reparation for the SINS by which He is offended, and in supplication for the conversion of SINNERS... Pray, pray very much and make sacrifices for SINNERS, for MANY SOULS go to Hell because they have nobody to pray and make sacrifices for them"-- Our Lady of Fatima.

Our Lady also assured us that "**Jesus wishes to establish in the world devotion to My Immaculate Heart.**" Such devotion or consecration is to be both personal and ecclesial.

"**I shall come to ask for the consecration of RUSSIA to My Immaculate Heart and the Communions of reparation...If My requests are fulfilled, RUSSIA will be converted and there will be peace. If not, RUSSIA will spread HER ERRORS throughout the world promoting wars, persecution of the Church, the good will be martyred...nations will be annihi-lated...**" -- Our Lady of Fatima.

What was the requested ecclesial consecration? That the Pope in union will all of the Catholic bishops of the world on one day consecrate RUSSIA to the Immaculate Heart of Mary.

The Fatima Message demands the **awesome Fatima consecrations.** This is God's will. In this book we will consider the Fatima Message, Challenge, Opportunity, Blessings and Consecrations as well as our responses to them.

Author's Note:

Where Gorbachev is referred to in the text of this book, it should be noted that this applies to Mr. Mikael Gorbachev or the present reigning dictator in Russia, whoever he currently is.

TABLE OF CONTENTS

Introduction

This book considers in depth the awesome meaning, relevance and necessity of these special Fatima consecrations - personal and ecclesial. We will see that in these end-times, GOD, through Our Lady of Fatima, has **demanded** that such consecrations be made in order to bestow upon us much-needed blessings and in order to help us to avoid horrible physical and spiritual punishments (both temporal and eternal).

The **primary** Fatima consecration is **personal.** YOU are called to consecrate (to make holy **with** or **by** God's grace and mercy in Christ Jesus) *yourself* according to God's command as given to you by Our Lady of Fatima.

In these end-times, you are to consecrate yourself to the Immaculate Heart of Mary and thus to the Sacred Heart of Jesus **or** you are to consecrate yourself to the Sacred Heart of Jesus through the Immaculate Heart of Mary - this is God's clear, emphatic and indisputable will (as will be proven to you).

The **secondary** Fatima consecration is **ecclesial.** The Pope "collegially" united with **all** of the Catholic bishops of the world is to consecrate RUSSIA (on the same day) to the Immaculate Heart of Mary and thus to the Sacred Heart of Jesus.

[IF such a consecration has not yet been accomplished (as of now, winter of 1991-92, the proper "Fatima demanded" ecclesial consecration has not been made), then God Himself has clearly promised that ever increasing physical and spiritual, temporal and eternal, individual and social PUNISHMENTS AND EVILS will be inflicted on mankind. However, *if* **such a consecration has finally been accomplished (after more than seventy-four years), then this book will motivate you to thank God for His many blessings which flow from the Pope and His bishops FINALLY doing the will of God.]**

Other "lesser" **ecclesial** consecrations are also recommended. For example, the Portuguese bishops consecrated their nation to the Immaculate Heart of Mary. Parishes and dioceses throughout the world have also been consecrated to the Immaculate Heart of Mary. Also, as a parent - especially as the head of the family, the father - you could consecrate yourself and your family to the Immaculate Heart of Mary. However, make sure you do so in spirit and in truth; in word and in deed; by your words and by your example.

Reading and praying this book will lead you to see the *"awesome* **necessity"** of making the Fatima Consecrations. Let the Holy Spirit direct you to *do* what Christ through Mary will lead you to do for the glory of the Father and for the temporal and eternal *well-being* of yourself and others.

This book is divided into five parts. First, a general background is presented. Then, we consider the **personal** Fatima consecration. In part three, we consider the **ecclesial** Fatima consecration as a call to action.

In part four, you will be led to make a **PERSONAL CON-SECRATION** (if you so desire and if God graces you to do so). In part five, you will be presented with a SAMPLING of the affirmations and denials which are implied **in** and **by** the **AWESOME FATIMA CONSECRATIONS** -- personal and ecclesial.

PART ONE

AN OVERVIEW

Introduction to Part One

In this first part, we consider three general areas - the nature of prophecy and Fatima as THE prophecy of our day; our recent history in the light of Fatima; and, "in house" rifts or divisions among those who claim to believe in or to "take seriously" the Fatima prophecy and challenge.

As we take up our considerations, realize that we are, for the most part, presuming that the **ecclesial** Fatima consecration has *not* been accomplished. *If* it has been accomplished, you can still profit by reading and praying this part of the book as it will help demonstrate the power of intercessory prayers over the obstinacy of our church leaders as well as lead you to see more clearly the curses which have come from disobedience and the blessings which have flowed from obedience.

Also (**if the** ecclesial consecration of RUSSIA has been properly done), by reading this book you will become more appreciative of the "power in" consecrating oneself or others to the Immaculate Heart of Mary. You will become "all the more" **inspired** to spread devotion and consecration to the Immaculate Heart of Mary. Such consecrations are truly **awesome**!

If the proper consecration of RUSSIA has been accomplished - you will see how the sinful disobedience of past Popes (and bishops) affected all of us (you will *see* the horror of sin); and, you will be ever more convinced of the great blessings that come from obeying God.

4

Special Foreword For
Part One

After proving (in chapter one) that Fatima's Message is authentic **God-given PROPHECY,** we will consider HOW the Catholic Church responded to God's Opportunity, Challenge and Blessing (chapters two through five). In order to be prepared for this type of study, you need to prayerfully consider and realize the following.

Cardinal Ratzinger, the Prefect for the Sacred Congregation for the Doctrine of the Faith, describes the present Catholic Church in one word -- **CRISIS.** The Church is in crisis.

The crisis affects all areas of Church life -- discipline, the teaching and transmission of doctrine, faith and morals, seminary training, general catechesis, imposed programs, national episcopal declarations, etc.

For most of my life, I spent too much time and effort looking in the **wrong direction** for the sources of the crisis as well as for solutions. I naively believed that the crisis came from the lower level, such as the clergy and bureaucrats within dioceses and national bodies. In effect, I believed that the crisis simply came from the fact that nations, dioceses and parishes refused to do what "Rome" wanted.

I even ventured so far as to consider the crisis and its "solution" to be residing in or coming from errant bishops. I was correct to some extent -- yet, the crisis originated far beyond any parish, diocese or nation.

I was enlightened by a devout practicing Catholic and blind psychiatrist, Dr. D.F. Carlos. In effect, he perceived that **a** (not, **the)** major cause of our grave crisis **COMES FROM "ROME"** (especially, for him in his prayer life, the "Rome approved" NOVUS ORDO Mass prayers).

This blind man saw far more than I did. "Rome" is at fault far more than most of us are willing to perceive.

The stigmatist and prophet, Anna Emmerich, foretold over a hundred years ago that **many clerics in our day would be excommunicated** -- whether or not they admitted it. She said that God's Truth as spoken by His Church remains true and that clerics who deny such truth are automatically in heresy. In effect, she "foretold" a "practical side" of the Fatima Message.

In studying and applying the Fatima Message, you will come to realize the **unpleasant** truth that in recent times, some (perhaps

5

most) Popes, cardinals, bishops, priests and even "the experts" have been horribly unfaithful to God. They have betrayed their God-given responsibilities. Some of them are gross sinners who **abide in a state of heresy.**

The Fatima Message and its application present you with a fundamental option. Either man sins or Reality (God's Revelations and His real Church) no longer exists or, at least, has something **substantially** wrong with it.

Your choice is similar to Celia's in THE COCKTAIL PARTY. Her paraphrased remarks are: "I should really **like** to think there's something wrong with **MEN**...or, if there isn't, then there's something wrong with **REALITY ITSELF** -- and that's much more frightening! That would be terrible (THE COLLECTED POEMS AND PLAYS OF T.S. ELIOT, Harcourt, Bruce and World, Inc., N.Y., 1952)."

The choice is yours. As for me, I choose God before MAN. I believe that there's something wrong with MEN -- rather than, with God and His Reality. If you are willing and "graced" to do the same, then part one (as well as part three) will not be threatening, but instead informative and helpful beyond your wildest dreams.

Also, if you are considerably uncomfortable with acknowledging that MEN -- Popes, cardinals, bishops, priests and even "experts" -- can be and are grossly sinful, then a third of this book will show you for what you are (even though, the chances are, you will remain blind to reality).

You are a **gross sinner and a psychotic.** You have been damned by God to be blind to the truth and to perceive error as truth and truth as error (cf. Rm. 1:18 -2:4). You have abandoned the Truth to embrace that which makes you feel good (II Ti. 4:3,4) within your own sinfully self-created unreal world (Gn. 6:5; 8:21).

Chapter One

Authentic Marian *Prophecy*

What is prophecy? What is Marian Prophecy? When is an alleged prophecy or apparition truly prophetic? Are alleged apparitions - such as those from Medjugorje or elsewhere - truly prophetic? Can an alleged apparition be profitable for you (and others) and **not** be truly prophetic? What must consecration to Mary be based on - visions and signs **or** God's true prophecies?

These important and timely questions - along with other related questions - will be answered in this chapter. Why? So that you can "believe" or firmly realize that the Fatima Message is one of the *very few* or the only prophetic utterance in recent times and that it is *THE* prophetic Marian message of the twentieth century. As such, it *must* be obeyed.

We will see that alleged apparitions or private "revelations" (or even "special personal happenings" at alleged holy places) which are **not prophetic** can still be conducive to one's salvation and **not** conducive to one's damnation if one follows certain criteria. These criteria can be perceived as you read this material. It must also be noted that **private** apparitions or locutions are also attributable to the preternatural or satanic.

Perhaps, the Virgin, in this age of internal and external apostasy, can only reach certain individuals by means of the spectacular. Those who are recipients of such graces, must always realize that **more** is required of them -- **they** must become clearly and authentically **holier** than others.

Prophecy

The prophet is here to correct abuses in the priesthood (the role of the priest will be presented later on). Also, the prophet speaks God's relevant message to us. As such, he elicits an "OUCH" [leading to an "Amen" for those who are to be saved (or to a clenched fist for those who will be damned)] OR the true prophet elicits an "AMEN" (from those who are "of" God the Father).

Yet, **how** does a true prophet prophesy? What does a true prophet prophesy? More importantly, for us, how can we recognize a true prophet? How can we tell the difference between a false prophet and a true prophet?

We look to God-proven prophecy -- the Bible -- for our answers. **The Bible tells us that any alleged prophecy must prove itself** to be true prophecy (according to the criteria that come from common sense and that God gives us in the Bible). Every alleged prophecy must prove itself to be truly from God and thus prophetic. As such, it is, or "becomes," **GOD'S WORD TO US.**

Here are the criteria for true prophecy:

1. Predictions are made. The short-term predictions come true (Jer. 28) or an **unquestionable** *and spectacular* miracle occurs as predicted or alongside of the predictions. **AND:**

2. All of the predictions and **their accompanying** *messages* must agree with the Bible (Ga. 1:8) -- or that part of it which is already in existence. As such they mirror man as he is - sinful; man as he can be through obeying God - saved; and, man as he will be by continuing to live in disobedience - damned and partaking of destruction, despair and death. Also, as Biblical, each message must conform to **authentic** Catholic teachings (Mt. 16:19).

Briefly stated (so far), true prophecy gives us a prediction that can be proven *and* a message that is Biblical (and thus Catholic -- in the true sense of the word).

There exists a third element or characteristic which defines prophecy to be truly prophecy: it must **ultimately,** at least, be *corrective and relevant. Thus:*

3. True prophecy "**makes relevant**" and **corrects.** There are two dimensions of church life - the priestly and the prophetic. The priestly dimension "re-presents," preserves and hands on faithfully and intact TRADITION (that which officially or "dogmatically" constitutes or defines the Catholic Church and before it was established by Jesus, the Jewish religion).

The true prophet highlights certain parts of AUTHENTIC TRADITION in order to make them relevant to the times in which the prophet lives.

The classical Old Testament prophets, as well as (of course) Jesus and the "post-Pentecost" apostles illustrate the role of a prophet before the second century, A.D. It might prove profitable for you to read some of them in order to see GOD'S criteria of prophecy "in action." It is interesting to note that as soon as the Catholic Church began its existence, God decreed that the prophetic must exist alongside of the priestly (as the authentic and faithful preservation, transmission and "living" of Catholic Tradition).

Mary is the Queen of Prophets. In these end-times, Her paramount role of being THE PROPHET (after Jesus and the Holy

Spirit, of course) is being made explicit and outstanding. So far, the Queen of Prophets has given us only one clear **and** outstanding prophecy - the **on-going** prophecy of Fatima (which continues until the death of Sister Lucy).

Lastly, remember no prophecy is **profitable for you or others** unless you and/or they prayerfully assimilate it and apply it to life. You apply prophecy by taking it to heart and by living it as well as by propagating it.

Marian Prophecy

Marian Prophecy is prophecy which comes from God through Mary. As authentic, such prophecy must include one or more predictions that clearly, spectacularly and convincingly come true and/or an indisputable and outstanding miracle. Also, the prophecy **must** be Biblical and agree with the core and authentic teachings of the real Catholic Church.

These end-times abound with **alleged** Marian prophecies. **Some** alleged prophecies (and, of course, alleged apparitions) are false and demonic (they emanate from the deceptive devil who duplicates "holy things" in order to disparage them). **Some** of them aren't prophecies; but, **private** visions - which may be spiritually beneficial or spiritually harmful, (which may emanate from God, "nature" or Satan).

A few alleged Marian prophecies are clearly authentic. Lourdes is authentic and culminates in Mary's declaration: "I am the Immaculate Conception." Lourdes was, as it were, *the* **Prelude to Fatima** - as far as prophecy is concerned. **Fatima is the fulfillment of Lourdes.**

FATIMA IS THE MARIAN PROPHECY OF OUR TIMES AND, POSSIBLY, OF ALL TIMES. FATIMA IS *GOD'S WORD* **TO MANKIND.**

Fatima is THE end-times Marian Prophecy. ALL of its clear and outstanding predictions have come true exactly as predicted. More than two *spectacular* public miracles happened just as predicted. *Finally*, since Fatima's message is not only *proven* but also Biblical and totally Catholic - it must be held *as being truly GOD'S WORD TO US.* As such, it *must* be obeyed.

Fatima is THE Marian Prophecy of modern times. As one ignores it, one ignores God. As one disobeys it, one disobeys God.

So far, all other subsequent prophecies are footnotes to Fatima

9

-- that is, if they are authentic. For example, the Ukrainian apparitions of 1987 seem to have been an enormous number of private visions (perhaps, 500,000 or more). In about half of these visions, Our Lady allegedly spoke to each individual. Her prophetic messages were merely footnotes to Fatima.

The Marian Messages and **Miracles** of the Ukraine stressed the importance of THE FATIMA MESSAGE. As it were, these apparently miraculous prophetic happenings provide us with additional confirmations of **THE** PROPHECY OF OUR DAY, FATIMA.

We must obey THE Marian Prophecy, Fatima.

In the Ukraine, Mary came once more "with tears in Her eyes." She reiterated a practical part of HER FATIMA MESSAGE: "Say the Rosary every day." She assured us of the urgency to obey the FATIMA COMMANDS (especially, those concerning our making and living the AWESOME FATIMA CONSECRATIONS) as She assured us that **indeed we are in the end-times.** Finally, She pleaded with us to **live and propagate the AWESOME FATIMA CONSECRATIONS: "LIVE IN TRUTH AND TEACH YOUR CHILDREN TO LIVE IN TRUTH."**

Another apparently authentic and "church approved" (at least, on the diocesan level) "mildly proven" Marian prophecy seems to have occurred in Akita, Japan (1973). This prophecy, along with "Akita," is a "CONFIRMING FOOTNOTE TO FATIMA." It emphasizes the urgent necessity of **our making and livng the awesome Fatima Consecrations.**

At Akita, the Blessed Virgin repeated the essential Fatima Challenge -- repent or be punished severely. She also asked for special prayers for priests, bishops and the Pope.

Why do they need these prayers? Many of them will abandon or betray Christ as they are led by the devils to do their work. They will spread demonic CONFUSION throughout the Church.

Also, we are told that if a sufficient number of us do not repent and, in effect, embrace the awesome personal Fatima Consecrations, the world will be punished in such a spectacular manner that the only hope that will be left for the miserable and suffering survivors will be "the Rosary and the Sign left by the Son of God."

The Ukrainian and Akita Marian messages, as well as any and all apparently authentic Marian messages do *not* replace Fatima. They underline the importance of Fatima. Fatima remains *THE* PROPHECY OF OUR DAY. OUR MAJOR GOD-GIVEN FATIMA CHALLENGE IS TO PERFORM

10

THE AWESOME FATIMA CONSECRATIONS -- BOTH PERSONAL AND ECCLESIAL.

Is Medjugorje Prophetic?

What about Medjugorje? There is, at present, **absolutely** *NO* **classical prophetic content to Medjugorje.** Perhaps, when the "apparent game" of ten secrets is ended, we will have a prophetic element with which to validate or reject Medjugorje. Therefore, Medjugorje has **ABSOLUTELY NO PROPHETIC VALUE.**

At present, it appears to be, from my point of view, an INSULT to Mary for Her to daily... weekly... monthly indulge in **CHIT-CHAT.** Furthermore, some alleged "**personal miracles**" at Medjugorje were subjected to scrutiny by the "Lourdes medical team" and all of them were found to be lacking in "authenticity."

Up to the present time, the local **Church authority,** Bishop Zanic, has investigated Medjugorje and, in effect, rejected it as being from God. He has done all he can to discourage and forbid its promotion (yet, "Rome," at times, does not seem to "back him up").

After carefully studying the Medjugorje phenomena within diocesan and national commissions, the Yugoslavian bishops in November, 1990, at Zagreb, concluded that they "cannot say that Medjugorje deals with supernatural apparitions or revelations." **A fortiori,** Medjugorje has absolutely **NO prophetic value** (according to regional episcopal authority) -- it isn't clearly and conclusively GOD'S WORD to us. **Lourdes and Fatima** *are* **prophetic -- in the true sense of the word -- NOT, MEDJUGORJE.**

Also, the lives of the seers in **no way** parallel those of Saint Bernadette of Lourdes and the holy children of Fatima. In fact, at the time of this writing one of them is a barmaid in Medjugorje.

So far, none of the alleged seers is leading an exemplary and outstanding holy life - which we could reasonably expect from those who daily... weekly... monthly...or bi-yearly have (or, had) a direct visit from Our Lady. Their comments are also filled with indications that they are **not** as holy as they should be in the light of what they claim to have witnessed.

Studies of Medjugorje indicate grave difficulties in "believing in it" as being truly from Mary and God; as being truly Biblical and Catholic. **Certainly, so far, at least, it is not TRULY AND "FULLY" PROPHETIC.**

However, "Medjugorje" seems to be **relatively valuable** to some Europeans and North Americans. We live in a horribly and

11

deceptively rotten and negative spiritual milieu.

Many of us who go to Medjugorje are quite impressed by the positive, sound and traditional spirituality that pervades in this section of Yugoslavia (especially, among the native clergy and laypeople). They are called to live their faith -- the liberal religion that our religious establishments "inflict on us" is unlivable in Reality (since it isn't really Catholic).

Also, **THINGS HAPPEN** to some people who go there. In as much as these "things" bring them closer to God and to Mary, they could be helpful towards **their** own personal salvation. The final test of **personal worth** will occur on their deathbeds -- but, in the short time in between, shouldn't you build your life on God's sure word and God's real prophecies? Don't build on sand!

In spite of all of the apparently (or, "possibly") good and positive aspects of Medjugorje, we must always remember that FATIMA, *not* Medjugorje, *is* indisputably proven prophecy. Listen to the FATIMA MESSAGE. Do what FATIMA says to do - both as regards personal consecration to Mary *and* as regards supporting and promoting the proper ecclesial consecration to Mary.

FATIMA is **THE** God-given prophecy. It is GOD'S very special prophetic WORD to us -- to you, to me and to everyone else who lives in these end-times. Absolutely nothing can, or should, replace FATIMA.

A Demonic Goal?

Is Satan **victorious in distracting you** from FATIMA and in reducing FATIMA'S importance to the level of **being one of several visions (which, in effect, you, as some sort of absolute judge,** can freely choose to ignore or to heed)?

Pray. "Back away." See the truth. At least, become, by God's grace, **objective to reality.**

Will not God lead you through any and all of your devotions to a greater devotion to His prophetically or "Biblicly" proven and totally authentic Marian prophecy, FATIMA? (FATIMA is *authentic* God-given prophecy -- as is evident to anyone who can SEE.)

The Fatima Message Or Prophecy Comes From God

The *major*, if not *only* significant God-given post-apostolic prophecy is FATIMA. Moreover, the Church has given Fatima its full approbation. Therefore we *must* believe and act on what it discloses. We must obey its consecration DEMANDS -- both personal and ecclesial. WE MUST OBEY GOD OR, WE WILL CONTINUE TO SUFFER HORRIBLE CONSEQUENCES: both temporal and eternal, both personal and social; and, both physical and spiritual.

FATIMA IS PROVEN PROPHECY. AS SUCH, IT IS GOD'S WORD TO US. AS SUCH, WE MUST BELIEVE IT AND OBEY ITS GOD-GIVEN MESSAGES.

A few of the FATIMA prophecies (or, more precisely, prophetic elements) and their fulfillments are given below. Try to realize the "unique-ness" of FATIMA. It is *PROVEN TO BE* GOD'S WORD TO US (which demands the awesome, yet simple, personal and ecclesial consecrations).

Generic Biblical Prophecies -- God appears to man in a cloud (*sheckinah glory*, Ex. 40). The end-times will happen within a setting of lightning, voices, earthquake and great hail (as predicted in Apoc. 12:19). In the last days, signs will appear "in the sun (Lk. 21: 25)."

FULFILLMENTS -- THE SEERS NOTICED A FLASH OF LIGHTNING BEFORE THE APPARITIONS (**SISTER LUCY'S MEMOIRS**). AT THE APPARITIONS, THE CROWD HEARD THE "BUZZING OF VOICES" (AS RELATED BY MARIA CARIERRA). ON AUGUST 13, 1917, THE GATHERED CROWD HEARD THUNDER, THEN THEY SAW LIGHTNING AND THE SPECIAL CLOUD DESCEND. AT THE GREAT MIRACLE OF OCTOBER 13, 1917, THE ENTIRE CROWD WITNESSED THE MIRACLE OF THE SUN (Lk. 21:25). THE SUN GYRATED...BROKE INTO COLORS AND PLUMMETED TO THE EARTH. MIRACULOUSLY, THE CROWD AND THE GROUND WERE BOTH DRY AFTER SEVERAL HOURS OF INTENSE RAIN.

WE NOTICE THAT GREAT HAIL IS ABSENT FROM FATIMA. WHY? THE HAIL OF CHAPTERS EIGHT, ELEVEN AND SIXTEEN (OF THE APOCALYPSE) IS PART OF THE **ACTUAL PUNISHMENTS** THAT GOD WILL INFLICT ON UNREPENTANT MANKIND -- FOR ITS FAILING TO

PROPERLY RESPOND TO THE FATIMA MESSAGE AND COMMAND.

Prophecy - "I will take Francisco and Jacinta soon." (June 13, 1917)

FULFILLMENT - THEY BOTH DIED WITHIN TWO AND A HALF YEARS.

Prophecy - Jacinta discloses in 1919 that "Our Lady told me I will go to the hospital in Lisbon, suffer much and die alone."

FULFILLMENT - IN 1920 THIS PROPHECY WAS FULFILLED EXACTLY.

Prophecy - Our Lady: "In October, I will perform a miracle so that all may believe (July 13, 1917)."

FULFILLMENT - 70,000 PEOPLE WITNESS THE MIRACLE OF THE SUN. THE "ANTI-CHURCH" PRESS REPORTS THE MIRACLE.

Prophecy - "The war is going to end (Our Lady, July 13, 1917)."

FULFILLMENT - WORLD WAR I'S FIGHTING ENDS NOV. 11, 1918.

Prophecy - "But if people do not cease offending God, another and more terrible war will break out during the reign of Pius XI (Our Lady, July 13, 1917)."

FULFILLMENT - HITLER STARTS HIS MONSTROUS AGGRESSION IN EUROPE MARKING THE BEGINNING OF W.W.II DURING THE PONTIFICATE OF PIUS XI. (BENEDICT XV WAS POPE DURING FATIMA APPARITIONS.)

Prophecy - "When you see a night illumined by an unknown light, know this is the great sign given you by God that He is about to punish the world...(Our Lady, July 13, 1917)."

FULFILLMENT -- AN UNEXPLAINABLE OR "UNKNOWN" LIGHT ILLUMINED THE NIGHT OF JANUARY 25th, 26th, 1938. THIS LIGHT HAS ALWAYS BEEN REGARDED BY SR. LUCY AS THE "FATIMA-PROMISED" GOD-GIVEN LIGHT WHICH WAS TO PRECEDE WORLD WAR II. (THIS SAME LIGHT WAS ALSO FALSELY INTERPRETED BY ADOLF HITLER AS A PROMISE OF SUCCESS.)

Prophecy - "If My requests are heeded, Russia will be converted ... if not, she will spread her errors throughout the world causing wars and persecution of the Church. The good will be

martyred, the Holy Father will have much to suffer, various nations will be annihilated (July 13, 1917)."
FULFILLMENT - REQUESTS HAVE NOT BEEN HEEDED AND RUSSIA'S ERRORS INCREASINGLY ENGULF US, ETC. ALSO, REMEMBER THAT RUSSIA AT THE TIME OF THIS PROPHECY WAS A WEAK AND BACKWARD NATION. SUCH A PROPHECY WOULD BE EQUIVALENT TO SOMEONE SAYING THAT BRAZIL WILL SPREAD ITS ERRORS THROUGHOUT THE WORLD.

Live In Truth

Build your house on the solid rock of God's revelations and God's prophetic utterances. **Don't** build on what appears to be a rock but what are really particles of sand temporarily glued together (by shifting emotions and/or deceptive signs and wonders).

In our day, **many** will be deceived (1 Tim. 4:1-2 and II Thes. 2:3-4). NOW is the time for **special caution** and *not* for "trusting and loving everyone."** NOW is **not** the time to "take chances" and follow signs and wonders. Some of these, we are assured by God, will lead you to Satan and to Hell (Mt. 24:9-13; 24).

Build on the Rock, Peter, **Christ's** one and only Church **and** on clearly proven prophecy. Don't be foolish. The Biblically consonant and totally authenticated messages of Fatima come through Mary and are from God. **God** speaks to us at Fatima and even beyond Fatima through "**the real**" Sister Lucy continuing to give us "Fatima messages" from Our Lord or Our Lady.

The authentic prophetic voice emanating from Fatima **demands** the consecration of Russia (as well as personal consecrations). **God** Himself demands that these consecrations be made to and through His Mother, Mary.

What is your attitude? What is your response? What is your awful responsibility - your accountability to God?

On December 26, 1957, Sister Lucy told Father Fuentes that Our Lady sadly spoke to her: "Father, the Most Holy Virgin is very sad, because nobody is concerned about Her message, the good as well as the evil. Tell them, Father, that the Holy Virgin has told me many times, as also Francisco and Jacinta that many people will be wiped from the face of the earth. She said that Russia will be the scourge, chosen by Heaven, to chastise the entire world if people do not obtain beforehand the conversion of THAT POOR NATION." *How* is such a conver-

15

sion obtained? As Sister Lucia told the Pope in 1929, by the consecration of RUSSIA to the Immaculate Heart of Mary by the Pope with the (Catholic) bishops of the world in union with him (or the Pope with HIS bishops) as well as by *your* devotion and consecration to Our Lady of Fatima.

The *proper* "Fatima" consecration of Russia is so very simple. Yet, it's an *awesome challenge.*

The same applies to **your** proper consecration to Mary. It's so very simple and awesome. Give your life to prayer, obedience to God, mortification, and conversion (coming to true faith or growing in faith).

Your personal consecration to Mary is called for by the authenticated and absolutely true prophecy of Fatima - THE prophecy for our day. Your personal consecration is simple. Yet, it's an **awesome challenge.**

Conclusion For Chapter One

Many alleged "Marian phenomena" fill our present world. How are we to react to them? This final section is of utmost importance -- it may be instrumental in saving YOU from eternal Hell. Meditate and pray about the following observations.

We are now living within a peculiar stage of the end-times. Satan has already managed to "trivialize and trash" **most** authentic Catholic "entities" (in the minds and hearts of most Euro-American "Catholics" and non-Catholics as surveys conclusively prove).

Concurrently, Satan has managed to "sensualize" most of us -- we live for/from the world and/or our flesh (our brains and/or bodies). However, we are and remain inherently or "naturally" meta-physical or "spiritual." We are starving for "the spiritual." We are post-Christian and pre-pagan.

Satan satisfies our hunger. He gives us the neo-pagan. He provides us with the pleasant, pious and spectacular (cf. II Thes. 2: 7-12). He deceives most of us as he skillfully combines modern scientific terminology, methodology and findings with the pagan [e.g. within "Catholicism," we have such "new things" as: enneagram retreats, certain liturgical practices, "Rogerianism" as supplanting dogma, liberal catechetical methodology and content; and, certain appealing and even spectacular "Marian" phenomena (which are built on or lead to an "unreal or even, crazy, Mary")].

In this peculiar phase of the end-times, it is quite urgent that you build your house on the **END-TIMES ROCK** which is composed of God's proven prophecies -- the Bible, its living fulfillment in the

16

real Catholic Church and the proven prophecies of Fatima.

Any other foundation which differs significantly from the END-TIMES ROCK is nothing but appealing and deceptive sand. Any such foundation will lead you to an eternal Hell.

Our peculiar test in this phase of the end-times is to realize and to admit that the "existential" church in many areas of the world and in many instances is corrupt. As Sister Lucy, the Seer of Fatima, observed about some of our clerical leaders: they are "dominated by a diabolic wave," they operate under a "diabolic disorientation," and they are disoriented, deceived and faithless. Consequently, some of them are "blind men leading the blind."

Such is the condition of a large part of the contemporary Catholic Church. Jesus predicted that these times would come (cf. Mt. 24). In this chapter of St. Matthew, Jesus Himself (in spite of our lying scripture scholars who claim we don't know what Jesus said and didn't say) said the following:

> **Men will hate, persecute and murder the few who follow the Truth and tell the truth (v.9). False prophets and false and deceptive prophecies will abound (v.ll). These prophets and prophecies will lead MANY to an eternal Hell (v. ll). These prophets and prophecies will be so enticing and overwhelming that, if possible, they would lead the very elect into Hell (v.24). Diabolic deception will be accompanied by pleasant, pious and spectacular signs and wonders (v.24).**

Indeed, the **END-TIMES ROCK** (especially, Fatima and Mt. 24) equips us for the peculiar trials of our day. A plethora of apparitions and alleged prophecies as well as prophets confront us. We are being betrayed by **men** -- even those who wear clerical garb.

Build your life on the **END-TIMES ROCK**. Let all of your devotions flow from and remain within **this ROCK**. Refuse to go beyond the boundaries or parimeters of this ROCK. Be convinced that pleasant and powerful deceptions abound in our times. They will lead you to an eternal Hell.

Chapter Two

Fatima Demands The Awesome Consecrations And Awesome Reparations

As has been shown, Fatima is authentic prophecy. As such, it is GOD'S word to us. Is it not as **valid** as the Bible?

At first, God "**allegedly**" spoke at Fatima. Then, God proved "**beyond any doubt**" that **HE** spoke - by clearly and spectacularly fulfilled prophecies (as well as by fulfilling the other criteria of authentic GOD-GIVEN PROPHECY). Therefore, we **must** believe "in Fatima."

Fatima is *THE POST-BIBLICAL PROPHECY*. It stands alone. It is unique. Only "Lourdes (the "prelude" to Fatima) and Fatima" have the POSITIVE APPROVAL of the Real Catholic Church (other prophecies, at best, are approved -- as containing nothing contrary to our faith).

Yet, as prophecy from God, Fatima has the **same** purpose and setting as the classical prophecies - especially those of the Old Testament. After all, Mary **is** the Queen of Prophets.

Classical prophecy (speaking forth from God) -- in both the Old and New Testaments -- speaks to a certain group of people and their community. It urges them to see by faith the awesome horror of their **sins**. The true prophecies of Lourdes and Fatima call the people to see by faith that the wages of **sins** are destruction, desolation and death.

Seeing sin and its effects is an essential message of Fatima. The Fatima children were given "faith to see." "**Faith** is the **evidence** of the unseen world (Hb. 2:2)." It "takes faith" to see that sin "causes" wars, persecutions of the church and of good people, annihilation of nations, famines, ... and especially the loss of souls as well as "grief" to Jesus and Mary. Also, the Fatima children were given a special gift of faith -- to see Hell as **the** eternally abiding effect of SIN.

It would **seem** ("objectively speaking") that the Pope and our bishops (along with most Catholics) can't and/or won't "**convincingly see**" by faith. Are they not a "faithless lot?" Do they not imitate the usual way that God's people responded to prophecy (as seen in the prophetic books)?

Therefore, for our own and for others' spiritual (and physi-

cal) *good, we* who have the God-given ability to see by faith --
by the light of the God-confired Fatima Message -- must pray
and properly pressure our faithless and/or unconvinced
leaders *to act* as if they see the truth or, preferably, to act from
God's gift of faith.

This is our awesome task. *We* -- those who have faith -- must
bring our leaders, by our prayers, sufferings and proper pressuring, to faith and/or to act or "to do" according to faith.

A Non-Catholic Example

Abraham Lincoln, **apparently** was a man of faith who **shames**
the **apparent** faithlessness of our Catholic leaders. As he witnessed the destruction, desolation and death of civil war, he, a man
of faith, turned to God in **reparation** to make a **consecration** of his
country to GOD.

**Consecration requires reparation. Reparation leads to con-
secration.** *God* **calls for REPARATION at Fatima. Reparation**
comes from **seeing sin and its effects - by faith. Reparation** l*eads
to*: **confession of sins to God, public acknowledgement of sin;
and, humble prayer, fasting and humilation. Reparation is
embraced from love of God, Mary, ourselves and others.**

Such is God's **command** given at Fatima. Not only does God
require the proper awesome ecclesial consecration of Russia, He
also **requires** that the day of consecration be **A DAY OF
REPARATION.**

Usually, I do **not** emphasize this since once we are blessed with
a Pope together with **his** bishops of like mind (and, of course, a
minimum understanding of prophecy and/or Fatima) - then, the
Pope together with **his** bishops will "naturally" be led to include
reparation and the recommendation of the "**First Saturdays** of
reparation."

The Catholic Church's Awesome Day of Ecclesially Consecrating Russia to the Immaculate Heart of Mary will also be a Day of
Reparation to the Immaculate Heart of Mary and to the Sacred Heart
of Jesus. (On this great and wonderful day, this humble and
obedient Pope along with His bishops will "naturally" confess and
make reparation for their gross sins of disobeying God's Fatima
Commands.)

Prayerfully read and re-read the prophets - both of the Old and
New Testaments. See how awesome reparation is included in
awesome consecration. Lastly, you may profit by "intellectually
perceiving" by way of contrast to Lincoln's apparent **faithfulness**

our present **faithlessness** - especially as it exists in the Pope and/or bishops and/or inactive laity. Read and pray about Abraham Lincoln's call for a day of National Humiliation, Fasting and Prayer.

Pray for an increase of faith. Pray that our Church leaders may soon be graced to imitate the example of Abraham Lincoln. In the midst of civil war, Abraham Lincoln issued the following proclamation:

Abraham Lincoln's Proclamation Of A Day Of Reparation And Consecration:

"...It is the duty of nations, as of men, to owe their dependence upon the overruling power of God, to confess their sins and transgressions, in humble sorrow, yet with assured hope that genuine repentance will lead to mercy and pardon, and to recognize the sublime truth, announced in Holy Scriptures and proven by all history, that those nations only are blessed whose God is the Lord:

"...In as much as we know that, by His divine law, nations, like individuals, are subjected to punishment and chastisement in the world, may we not justly fear that the awful calamity of civil war, which now desolates the land, may be but a punishment inflicted upon us for our presumptuous sins, to the needful end of our national reformation as a whole people?...

"It behooves us, then, to humble ourselves before the offended Power, to confess our national sins, and to pray for clemency and forgiveness.

"Now, therefore, in compliance with the request, and fully concurring in the views of the Senate, I do, by this my proclamation, designate and set apart THURSDAY, the 30th day of April, 1863, as a day of National Humiliation, Fasting and Prayer. And I do hereby request all the people to abstain in that day from their ordinary pursuits, and to unite at their several places of public worship and their respective homes, in keeping the day holy to the Lord, and devoted to the humble discharge of the religious duties proper to that solemn occasion.

All this being done, in sincerity and truth, let us then rest humbly in the hope, authorized by the Divine teachings that the united cry of the Nation will be heard on high, and answered with blessings, no less than the pardon of our national sins, and restoration of our now divided and suffering country to its former happy condition of unity and peace."

Awesome Consecration:
Overwhelming Cure

What hope is there? Are we not involved in a perpetually worsening spiral?

Yes, we are **DE**scending spiritually. The **spirit** that prevails in Rome and throughout much of the "Catholic" world is faith-less and thus demonic. Reparation and consecration (which were part and parcel of the spiritual atmosphere in Lincoln's time) are **totally alien** to our spiritual atmosphere.

What is the cure? What is the restorative and health producing "food?"

On the personal level - our enduring cure lies in the following: prayer, particularly the Rosary, repentance, sacrifice, obedience, conversion to God, and *proper* action - reparation and consecration. On the ecclesial level, we *add* - admission of gross faithlessness, horrible cowardliness, etc. on the part of the "establishment church" along with a proper act of ecclesial **REPARATION** and ecclesial consecration to Truth through the proper ecclesial consecration of Russia to the Immaculate Heart of Mary as required by *GOD* at Fatima.

On the "divine level," God is led to do one or more of the following: punish the Church for its "most horrible" sins by persecutions and unimaginable sufferings, punish the world since His Ministers (the Pope and the Bishops) have delayed and disobeyed (as Fatima teaches), punish His Pope and higher clergy (not only in eternity, but here on earth as well), bring His higher clergy to admit their grossly horrible and heinous sins of failure and faithlessness (by sufferings and grace), lead His Pope to make reparation for his "most-awesome" sins of omission; lead His Pope together with the Pope's bishops to do the proper awesome reparations and consecrations and thus to grant peace, unity, proper government and order to His Church throughout the world (and THUS to bless the world).

There is HOPE. It is late. It will be even LATER - when proud and sinful higher clergy (and especially, the Pope) are led to humbly obey GOD'S DEMANDS. Yet, it is NEVER TOO LATE. In the end, the proper awesome consecration of Russia will be done and THUS a period of peace will be granted to the world - so promises Mary, the Mother of God and our Mother.

22

Papal Reparation And Papal Consecration

It is interesting to note that in the "on-going" prophecy of Fatima, that in August, 1931, Our Lord complained to Sr. Lucy about the disobedience of the Popes: **"They did not wish to heed MY DEMAND. Like the king of France THEY WILL REPENT and do it, but it will be late."**

What did Our Lord, Jesus Christ, prophesy? **THEY WILL REPENT.**

One Pope will come along and in union with **HIS** bishops will **REPENT.** He will see **SIN.** He will admit that **HE,** his predecessors and the Church have erred. He will confess apparent sin. He will **REPENT OF HIS APPARENT SINS** and be led to make **REPARATION.**

REPENTANCE LEADS TO REPARATION. REPARATION LEADS TO CONSECRATION. FINALLY, CONSECRATION REQUIRES THAT ONE "CONTINUALLY" SEES AND CONFESSES HIS SINS, REPENTS AND MAKES REPARATION.

We are assured that one day a Pope will cooperate with God's graces and admit that he has **sinned:** *"mea culpa, mea culpa, mea maxima culpa."* Such a Pope will imitate King David in his humble acknowledgement of **SIN** and consecration to **GOD AND GOD'S WILL.** Such a Pope will be so great as to imitate the humility and dedication to God that we perceive in Abraham Lincoln.

This man, as the Pope, will make reparation for his sins, the sins of his church and the sins of others. As Pope, he will gratefully and sincerely lead **his** bishops to make the proper Fatima ecclesial consecration of **RUSSIA** and to call for reparation (as Our Lord **commanded** at Fatima through Our Lady).

An American "Ecclesial" Illustration Of The Necessity Of Reparation

Almost coincidental with the Silver Anniversary of the infamous **Roe v Wade** U.S. Supreme Court decision which legalized murder, the American bishops belatedly issued a "disagreement." However, in effect, their disagreement was a political or politico-religious disagreement (to put it **"strongly"**).

The **apogee** in their 1989 statement was reached as they

proclaimed: "No Catholic can responsibly take a 'pro-choice' stand." Did not this rather mild episcopal stand amount to a political stand? Did not these bishops betray their God-given "magisterial responsibility?"

Why did the bishops wait until the FALL OF 1989 to issue such a statement? Morals don't evolve or change. Only politics changes.

Abortion is MURDER. It didn't become murder in 1989. Also, **de facto,** abortion is such "horrible murder" that one is excommunicated for procuring an abortion.

Moreover, the bishops (as a national body) cannot excuse their own "condemning silence" which stretched over a period of twenty-five years by claiming that the issue wasn't relevant (especially in view of the fact that less significant and even "immoral" issues were more strongly addressed and "enforced"). Certainly, these twenty-five years were relevant to the forty million victims of abortions and to the more than sixty million cold-blooded, yet legalized, murderers.

Not only was their 1989 statement **sinfully mild**, it also proved to be hypocritical. [As far as we can tell, many bishops worked behind the scenes to legislate abortion in certain cases (cf. issues of **The Wanderer** in 1990 and 1991). Certainly, direct abortion for any reason is always murder, or is it like "Catholic" divorce? Are not certain types of divorces when they are officially decreed to be annulments no longer to be considered to be divorces?] Why were the bishops' efforts in vain or even sinful? **They failed to embrace the SPIRIT OF FATIMA.**

THE SPIRIT OF FATIMA demands that the bishops perceive their past sins (at least, of silence) regarding abortion, admit such sins publicly (since they affected the public welfare), do public penance, MAKE REPARATION and resolve to sin no more. Then and only then, will they be graced to (and be able to) consecrate themselves in truth and to the Truth through the Immaculate Heart of Mary. Only then will they be able to do their God-given duty regarding abortion and all other critical issues.

Of course, this "spirit of Fatima" is also found in one's properly functioning conscience, in God's word, the Bible, and in the fundamental teachings of the real Catholic Church. This spirit is found in the awesome Fatima Message as it assures our spiritually blind and "self-justifying" generation that **sin** is not alien to the human dimension -- even to the human dimension of Popes and bishops. **Sin is "natural" to every man. Therefore, Fatima demands**

reparation and *then* consecration.

However, the bishops failed to heed the message of Fatima. Therefore, God gave them up to ineffectiveness, failure and sin. God gave them up to becoming politicians and **thus, for them,** to becoming sinners.

What **would have happened** had the bishops embraced the **SPIRIT OF FATIMA WHICH DEMANDS REPARATION ?**
At least the bishops would have been graced to do the following:
(l) They would have publicly confessed their gross sins of omission and inadequate action. They would have repented.
(2) They would have done penance for these sins. They would have imitated Abraham Lincoln in proclaiming a season of humiliations, fasting and prayers in the hope that God would forgive them their horrible **sins.**

"It is the duty of all men, and especially of bishops, to confess their 'social' sins sincerely and in humble sorrow; yet, with assured hope that **genuine** repentance will lead to receiving God's grace and mercy (as shown to us in the Fatima vision at Tuy). Therefore, we, the bishops of the United States of America, embrace and proclaim a season of special penance in which we invite you, our fellow priests and the faithful, to join us. We pray and do penance in the hope that God will answer us and grant us the grace to be consecrated in truth to Truth through the Immaculate Heart of Mary. Only then can we become that which we are obliged to be -- the light of this world."
(3) They would have issued a series of three or more "suggested" sermons to be given by priests on abortion [as they **did** in order to impose upon the faithful the practice of receiving Holy Communion in one's hand (which has proven to be a "spiritual failure")].
(4) They would have encouraged and urged pastors in every church to do their **GOD-GIVEN DUTY.** Pastors are **clearly empowered** by church law (canon 915) to refuse Holy Communion to "manifest sinners" such as doctors, legislators, nurses and other public figures who directly help others to procure abortions. "Those who persist in manifest sin are not to be admitted to Holy Communion (canon 915)."
(5) They would have been consecrated in truth to Truth. They would have done all in their power to have **God's will done on earth according to His heavenly plan. They would have been GOD'S MEN and not "MEN'S MEN."**

Indeed, the example of the American bishops points out to us the "urgent relevance" of the Fatima Message, especially, in its demand for **reparation.** Reparation is a prerequisite for consecration. Without sincere reparation, one's consecration or dedication to Truth is "damned to be" spurious and hypocritical.

Special Reparation

As we continue in disobedience, reparation becomes ever more difficult. Some will be required to (as well as, be graced to) make reparation from positions of extreme poverty, persecutions and misfortunes (misfortunes so extreme, in some, if not **many,** cases as to result in horribly painful deaths). Their sins and the sins of others will bring many to "extremes." At Fatima, God promised that ever worsening punishments are in store for human beings because of their ever growing gross disobedience to THE GOD-GIVEN PROPHECY OF FATIMA.

As it were, more and more will be led to suffer the agonies of crucifixion. In such agonies, they will have to choose a negative response or a positive response.

As they choose "negatively," they will join the "bad thief" on his cross and continue in sinfulness -- refusing to be humble, refusing to embrace "self-condemning" truth, cursing God, etc. and eventually dying in their sins. In effect, they will reject the awesome message of Fatima.

OR, as they choose "positively," they will join the "good thief" on his cross and come to embrace the **spirit of Fatima, a spirit of reparation and consecration.** With the good thief, they will admit their **sins,** accept their "well deserved punishments," and turn to God for grace and mercy (as depicted at the Fatima vision of Tuy). Do all you can to avoid being put in this special condition in which repentance and reparation will become more difficult. As you are graced to do so, make reparation for your past sins. Then, be consecrated to the Immaculate Heart of Mary.

Help Bring About The Proper Ecclesial Fatima Consecration

To be sure, reparation leads to consecration. Also, consecration leads one to live a life dedicated to reparation. One comes to consider others as more important than himself (cf. Phlp.2). One comes to consider the Hearts of Jesus and Mary as being of prime importance.

Then, one is impelled to pray for God's graces that will lead the

Pope to do God's will as expressed at Fatima. Our Lord assures us that one day the Pope will repent (of disobeying the God-given Fatima Command). Our Lady assures us that when a sufficient number make and live the Fatima Consecration, God's "overwhelming" graces will be bestowed upon the Pope and he will make the proper ecclesial Fatima Consecration.

However, don't stop with prayer. If you can, push and pressure the Pope and bishops to do what God wants to be done.

"Lead and encourage" them to become conscious of sin and thus of the need for reparation. Then, the desire for consecration -- both personal and ecclesial -- will follow.

The salvation of souls and their ease of salvation depends on our working and praying in order to have the Pope obey the Fatima Command. We work and pray with the assurance of victory.

One glorious and wonderful day in the future the Pope will **finally obey GOD'S COMMANDS AS GIVEN AT FATIMA.** Our Lord and Our Lady of Fatima assure us that one Pope, one day, will bring **his bishops** to join him in sincerely confessing: *"mea culpa, mea culpa, mea maxima culpa,"* and **then** making the proper Fatima ecclesial consecration of Russia.

You and I can help create this "atmosphere of **repentance and reparation."** Most likely, such an atmosphere is needed in order to lead the Pope into doing God's will as expressed at Fatima.

Abraham Lincoln, one of history's great leaders, embraced a spirit of repentance and reparation. He was probably "graced to do so" by living in an "atmosphere of repentance and reparation." Within such an atmosphere, it was easy for Abraham Lincoln to call for a day of repentance and reparation as he declared and decreed a day of humiliation, fasting and prayer.

In such an atmosphere, was he not "graced to see" that the awful calamity of civil war was "a **just and well-deserved God-given punishment** inflicted upon us **for our presumptuous SINS,** to the needful end of our national reformation as a whole people?" Can we not expect our Pope to receive similar graces?

Will not God lead the Pope to see the "uttermost" horror of **SIN** and **DEMAND** that his bishops join him in making **THE AWESOME FATIMA ECCLESIAL CONSECRATION OF RUSSIA TO THE IMMACULATE HEART OF MARY?** Are not repentance and reparation the prelude to consecration?

The Fatima ecclesial consecration will be done -- but, it will be done LATE. [Just *"how late"* **depends on our prayers and proper actions.]**

In the end, the Pope will be graced to obey GOD and will obey

God by doing as God commanded at Fatima. The awesome ecclesial Fatima consecration will be done and done properly. The Immaculate Heart of Mary will triumph.

CONSEQUENTLY, a period of true peace will be granted this world. [The Fatima Message assures us that true peace can **only exist** when God's one and only true church is true to God. Then, individuals of good will, will attain and live in true peace as they come to or return to (and consequently **abide within**) GOD'S one and only church in a spirit of repentance, reparation and consecration.]

So far, however, how has the Pope and "Rome" responded to the Fatima Commands, Challenges, Blessings and Opportunity? The next chapter will answer this question.

Chapter Three

The Ecclesial Fatima Consecration -- This God-Given Prophetic Challenge Is Responded To By Sinful Cover-Ups

The Blessed Virgin appeared at Lourdes (1858) to prepare mankind for Fatima and thus for this century and beyond. She emphasized **sin** as the ultimate and only evil and our need to be humble, do penance and come to the saving waters of the Catholic Church.

Pope Leo XIII, Pope St. Pius X and Pope Pius XI stand out in history as the Popes of the modern era who prepared the church and the world for our day. It would be worthwhile for you to glance through or even selectively study the encyclicals and other pronouncements of these outstandingly "prophetic" Popes.

The year, 1917 was a crucial year. As it were, **this** year not only "predicted the future," it also "controlled the future." This was the year of **three great events: the Fatima Message, the conception of Israel and the birth of "Red Russia."**

At Fatima, God prepared us for "Red Russia." At Fatima, God also gave us the **ABIDING REMEDY FOR "RED RUSSIA."**

At Fatima, God also prepared us for the end-times which were "conceived" as Israel was conceived. At Fatima, God gave us the **ABIDING REMEDY AND VICTORY FOR THESE END-TIMES -- THE AWESOME FATIMA CONSECRATIONS.**

The major Fatima apparitions to the three children occurred monthly from May 13, 1917 to **October 13, 1917.** On **October 17, 1917,** the Bolshevik Revolution gave birth to Red Russia. On **November 2, 1917** the Balfour Declaration "conceived" Israel and in doing so (in an effective manner), it indicated that the completion of the times of the Gentiles was "at hand (Lu. 21:24, Rm. 11:25)."

These are the end-times -- as Our Lady has assured us. The Political Beast of the end-times (the New Age Government) can now come upon the stage of history (Rv. 13: 1-10). The Religious Beast of the end-times (the New Age Religion) can now come upon the stage of history (Rv. 13: 11-18). As Cardinal Ratzinger and Sister Lucy observed about the Fatima Message -- it's all in the Bible, especially Revelations chapters eight to thirteen.

God's major concern is about **HIS** church -- the Catholic Church. It, and it alone, determines the chronology of the end-times. How does the Catholic Church determine the end-times? By its obedience to God or by its continuing disobedience.

When Red Russia (even though the colors of its flag may change, Russia remains RED Russia) is consecrated properly, then God will bless mankind. Red Russia can only be consecrated properly by the Pope together with **HIS** bishops. Until the Pope with His bishops obeys God, we will continue to suffer -- temporally and eternally, physically and spiritually; individually and socially.

Furthermore, you and I determine blessings or curses for mankind. When a sufficient number of individuals make and live the awesome personal Fatima consecrations; then, the Pope will be given "more than sufficient" graces to obey God and not MAN.

As the "existential" or "establishment" church continues to prefer MAN to God, it increasingly becomes a major part of the New Age Religious Beast. It can only be freed from such an abomination of desolation if it decides to obey God and make the **awesome ecclesial Fatima Consecration.**

Fatima's Consecration Challenges

Fatima, THE prophecy of our day, presents two challenges - one personal and the other ecclesial. Fatima calls for two major consecrations - personal and ecclesial.

In effect, **you** are challenged to consecrate **yourself** to Mary. Since She is **sinless**, in consecrating yourself to Her, you are, **de facto**, consecrating yourself to Jesus. The nature of such a consecration will be considered in part two.

Also, quite clearly, the Church (the one and only true church, the Catholic Church) is called upon in its priestly role (as "representing" man to God and God to man) to consecrate RUSSIA to the Immaculate Heart of Mary.

WHO is to do this consecration? **NOT** the people of the Church (**they** are **not** the priestly essence of Catholicism). The **Pope** - Christ the High Priest's Vicar on earth - (**together with HIS bishops**) represents and is the "highest Priestly essence" of Christ's true Church.

What a tribute to the Pope (and bishops)! What an honour! What an opportunity to praise God and to bless mankind!

So you may think: "Where's the problem?" **The Fatima Consecration is simple but also AWESOME.** It requires and demands a faith and holiness which the Pope (and bishops) lack.

Also, it requires a detachment from and a rejection of THIS WORLD which the Pope **doesn't** seem to possess.

The Mystery Of The Church: Divine; Yet, Human

It might prove profitable at this point to realize that the Church is a mystery. For example, the Pope can and does **sin** -- yet, as it were, in his **purely official** ""church-defining" role, he is sinless. Also, as Jesus stated about the sinful "cardinals and bishops" of His day - listen to or obey them (in their **official** capacity), but **don't** imitate them or obey them in their "unofficial-ness."

BY GOD'S GRACE AND THEIR GRACED COOPERATION, holy and wise Catholics make all of the necessary distinctions so that they can FAITHFULLY live within the mystery of a divine, yet human, Church. They "disobey" and ignore -- where such is appropriate. They obey and agree -- where such is appropriate. **They** not only survive in a wicked church, they also prosper in such a church.

While holy and wise (by the gift of the Holy Spirit) Catholics make all of the necessary relevant distinctions, most "Catholics" are faced with a test that many of them fail. In effect, they are tempted to adore MAN as God.

Apparently, they believe that man -- in the form of a Pope, bishop, priest, an "expert," etc.-- must be sinless (as far as they can perceive or be deceived into perceiving). They lack faith -- faith which will allow them to see and to realize that in certain circumstances or situations, God can operate through a sinful person: even, a sinful Pope.

Another problem emerges. As it were, GOD has a problem. As HIS Church becomes extremely sinful, as it *is* today, its divine characteristics are in danger of being obfuscated and suppressed.

A wicked church fails to show forth and make accessible the **HOLINESS** of the true Church. A pluralistic church fails to show forth the **UNITY** of the true Church. A faithless and faith-denying church fails to show forth the **APOSTOLIC** nature of the true Church. Finally, a church regionally defined by experts OR by "communities" fails to show forth the **CATHOLICITY** or "universality" of the true Church.

Yet, we **profess** the true faith - "I believe in **ONE, HOLY,**

31

CATHOLIC and APOSTOLIC Church." God has a problem.

How does He solve the problem? How has He solved such a problem? In the days of classical Old Testament prophecy, God called His Church to REFORM or to be **punished severely** -- here and in eternity. In our day, the Queen of Prophets has spoken this classical message at FATIMA. **REFORM OR BE PUNISHED!**

God's only apparent answer to His problem is TO PURIFY HIS CHURCH. How? By horrible punishments. THIS is the message of Fatima. REFORM OR BE PUNISHED SEVERELY!

"Make and mean" the personal and ecclesial consecrations OR be punished **severely** - temporally and eternally. Such is our AWESOME challenge.

Papal Victims

Regarding the ecclesial consecration, many of us have wondered why the Popes who reigned after 1917 didn't comply with Our Lady's demands. Communication wasn't as reliable and swift as it is today. Also, before 1960, the Popes were limited by their staffs as to what they "received from the outside world."

The "diabolic disorientation" that Sister Lucy speaks of prevailed from 1917 on. However, I contend that the Popes before Pope John XXIII were **victims** of this disorientation rather than participants in it.

For example, Pope Pius XII, who was quite devoted to Fatima, seemed to have been purposely misinformed about it. He was a **victim** of a cover-up or of lies about Fatima.

The famous Jesuit historian, Robert Graham, shocks us with his claim that Pope Pius XII consecrated the world and not **Russia** to the Immaculate Heart of Mary on October 13, 1942 because he was a **victim** of deliberately contrived misinformation (cf. **30 DAYS,** March, 1990). Two "Vatican-published" books replaced "Russia" and "Russia's errors" with "impious propaganda." Also, these authoritative books replaced the demand for the **consecration of Russia** with a demand for the **consecration of the world.**

We also contend that in 1942 when requested by the Holy See as to what the Pope should do to comply with Our Lady's demands, Don Jose, on his own authority, **combined** Alexandrina da Costa's (a local mystic, seer and "revered saint") request with the Fatima Message and thus told the Pope that Our Lady wanted **the world** to be consecrated to Her.

Therefore, we can see why on March 25, 1984, Pope John Paul

II **again** consecrated the world and **not Russia**. Established traditions are difficult to ignore -- especially, in Rome.

Therefore, I contend, we could possibly "excuse" the Popes before Pope John the Twenty-third. They could be victims, not victimizers.

Why does the "establishment-church" from 1960 on, so persistently not only disobey God but also try to justify their disobedience by issuing and enforcing "**cover-ups?**" I contend that the answer to this question can be traced back to the VATICAN-MOSCOW ENGAGEMENT (which was followed by a marriage and the birth of a child -- the presently enduring "glasnost").

Vatican-Moscow Engagement

In order to adequately understand the opposition to the ecclesial Fatima Consecration, one must realize that in 1962 the Vatican became engaged to Moscow (the Vatican-Moscow Agreement was made). Pope John the Twenty-third proudly wanted schismatic **Russian** Orthodox "bishops" at **his** council. He also feared Russia and desired peace "at Russia's price."

Lastly, according to Malachi Martin (who received his information from involved ecclesiastics), the **Third Secret of Fatima** which was read by Pope John the Twenty-third insisted that the Pope consecrate **Russia** to the Immaculate Heart of Mary **along with** the Catholic bishops of the world (otherwise, nations would lose the faith and cardinals, bishops and priests fall into hell like leaves falling from a tree).

Pope John the Twenty-third realized that such a consecration labelled Russia as evil and sinful. Russia specificly was in God's view in need of "an exorcism." The Pope feared that Kruschev would take such an act as an insult or even a "declaration of war." It appears that John the Twenty-third loved and feared MAN more than God.

Subsequent Popes joined him and "sold out" Mary for Moscow. In exchange for worldly peace and "ecumenical unity," Popes trampled on Fatima, disobeyed God and insulted the Blessed Virgin Mary as they promised to be faithful to Red Russia (and now, the emerging New Age One World Government and Religion) and not to God and Mary.

That's also the reason why the Second Vatican Council failed to issue a condemnation of the worst enemy of God not only in our day, but also in the history of mankind -- **communism or, in Our Lady's terms, RUSSIA'S ERRORS.** (It may prove helpful for you to carefully read **Gaudium et Spes** (77-93), Pope Paul VI's United Nations' speech, and the **Novus Ordo Mass** - with the Vatican-Moscow mindset in view.)

Our preferential love of Russia, MAN and the New Age is one major reason why we now have the **Fatima cover-ups.** Yet, there's hope. Our Lady assures us that the ecclesial Fatima Consecration will be done **LATE** and a period of peace will come to mankind. Until the ecclesial consecration is done - **the time will be LATE but never TOO LATE.**

Five Stages To The Fatima Ecclesial Consecration Cover-Up

[An evil "mega-power" operates **within** the Church --especially, **within** the Vatican itself. This power has decided not only to disobey God's Fatima Command, but also to try to justify its disobedience. This power issued the "**company lie**" in the FALL of 1989. THEY issued **THE FATIMA COVER-UP.**

For those who are not familiar with the present "cover-up," the following is presented. Notice that in stage **four** many important people involved "in" Fatima -- either "officially" or as "experts" -- agreed that, clearly and without any doubt, the Papal consecration of the world on March 25, 1984 was **NOT** the required **ecclesial** consecration of **RUSSIA** as demanded by God at Fatima.

In stage **five** many of these **same** "involved people" astonishingly changed their "**SPEECH.**" Obviously, a "cover-up" of the highest magnitude exists and flourishes within the Church.]

I. CONSECRATION OF RUSSIA TO THE IMMACULATE HEART OF MARY -- BY THE POPE IN UNION WITH THE CATHOLIC BISHOPS OF THE WORLD -- DEMANDED BY GOD THROUGH OUR LADY OF FATIMA IN 1917 AND 1929.

II. BETWEEN 1929 AND 1984, CONSECRATIONS WERE DONE -- YET NONE OF THEM COMPLIED WITH GOD'S DEMANDS REGARDING RUSSIA. THEREFORE, RUSSIA'S ERRORS SPREAD THROUGHOUT THE WORLD ALONG WITH WARS, PERSECUTIONS AND MUCH SUFFERING.

III. IN ROME, ON MARCH 25, 1984 THE POPE, AFTER SENDING AN INVITATION TO THE BISHOPS TO JOIN

HIM -- CONSECRATED THE WORLD, NOT RUSSIA, TO THE IMMACULATE HEART OF MARY.

This consecration became the object of a "cover-up" **some five years** after it was done -- even though: (1) it was of the **world** and not of **Russia**; (2) it was not done with **all of the Pope's bishops.** **In fact,** Sister Lucy testified that **"many** bishops did not attach any importance to it."

IV. FROM THE CONSECRATION OF 1984 TO THE FALL OF 1989:

A. Pope John Paul II twice admitted that the Russian people **still awaited** "their" consecration -- "enlighten especially those people **who are still awaiting** our consecration."

B. Sister Lucy on more than five occassions stated emphatically and clearly that the required consecration of RUSSIA was **NOT** done.

C. Quite a number of Cardinals -- such as, Law, Mayer, Stickler and Ratzinger -- stated that the required consecration of **Russia** was **NOT** yet done.

D. Maria do Fetal and others who spoke with Sister Lucy stated that the required consecration of RUSSIA was **NOT** done.

E. The great expert on Fatima, Fr. Messias Dias Coelho, from 1984 to 1989 in his newsletter **"MENSAGEM DE FATIMA"** assured us that the ecclesial consecration was **NOT** done. (Then, in 1989, he assured us that it **was** done.)

V. FROM THE FALL OF 1989 TO THE PRESENT (THE WINTER OF 1991), THE CONSECRATION "COVER-UP" HAS BEEN IN EFFECT. Why? We are "in the years of special **Perestroika."** We now live **A.P.** (in the years of Perestroika) -- as we await **the dawning of the New Age.**

THEREFORE, after the **FALL OF 1989,** the "party-line" or the "company lie" replaces the truth. To varying degrees and in "varying lack of clarity and/or conviction," the Pope, some cardinals, Sister Lucy, Maria do Fetal and others NOW apparently adhere to the "party line". A number of the above persons repeat the comforting **lie** -- RUSSIA was consecrated as God demanded through Our Lady of Fatima on March 25, 1984.

"Peace and unity" are now promised to MAN by MAN. The truth about Fatima and our failure to obey God -- must be suppressed, denied and covered-up with lies.

We must also note at this point that since we are involved with a **cover-up** which includes many famous and even (apparently) holy people, we can expect "slips" or disclosures of the **truth**. Maria do Fetal on one occassion returned to her original position or to **the truth** -- Russia was **not** consecrated as it should have been by the Pope on March 25, 1984. I contend that probably the Pope or Cardinal Ratzinger will finally come to admit that forces in the Vatican have issued and enforced **THE GREAT FATIMA COVER-UP.**

From 1989 To- ???? --
Years Of The Cover-Up:

As we have already noted, Sister Lucy on at least **five** occassions **before** the fall of 1989 emphatically and clearly stated the Consecration of Russia had **never** been done **as** Our Lady of Fatima requested (her last statement, as far as I know, came through her niece, Maria do Fetal in the summer of 1989).

The Pope, even on the day of the alleged Consecration of Russia, (**March 25, 1984**, the Consecration of the **WORLD** as made at the Vatican), admitted that Russia was **not** consecrated as God desired: "Enlighten especially the peoples whose consecration and entrustment by us **You are awaiting.**"

Then came **Perestroika** and **Glasnost** (the sixth in Russia's history). In 1989, Gorbachev was proclaimed the **Global Master** and given **Time's** 1990 Man of the Year Award together with the Nobel Peace Prize for 1990. The man who caused the Gulf Crisis of 1990 was given the Peace Prize (love blinds one to seeing the truth about the loved one).

Rejoice! Unto Us A Child Was Born.

The Vatican-Moscow agreement had its first child - **Glasnost Perestroika Vatican-Moscow (born in 1989).** Let no one dare to criticize **the fruitful marriage.** Unto us a child is born. Unto us salvation is given.

Therefore, the mega-power in the Church decreed a new formula for UNITY and FAITHFULNESS. One must believe the party-line - **Russia** was consecrated as Fatima desired in 1984. After all, Russia is part of the world and the Pope did **invite** the bishops to join him (although Sister Lucia protested: "**Many bishops did not give any importance to it**"). **Let no one dare to claim that the first child is illegitimate and not blessed by God**

and Fatima.

After the **conception** of **Glasnost** was discerned - sometime in 1989 - **apparently** the Pope, Sister Lucy, a few cardinals, and bishops, Father Robert Fox and a few experts changed their minds - or rather, **their speech.**

The new party line was New Age Unity, Peace and Safety as we follow the Red Dragon into a Heaven on Earth. However, to follow the Dragon, we must abandon Our Lady of Fatima -- in spirit as well as in truth.

Some of the questions that are presented in this book are: Why are the Fatima Consecrations (especially, the ecclesial Fatima Consecration) so threatening? Why do individuals and Christ's one and only true Church not only ignore Fatima but also oppose it to the extent of covering it up in reassuring **LIES - that the World is Russia and that a non-collegial consecration is a collegial consecration (in Mary's sense of the word** "collegial" **-- the Pope actually united with all the Catholic bishops of the world on one day)?**

The Third Secret
And The Ecclesial Fatima Consecration

As we have seen, according to Malachi Martin (who obtained his information from "reliable sources"), **the Third Secret** insisted on the ECCLESIAL FATIMA CONSECRATION being made. It also concerned the loss of faith and the eternal damnation of cardinals, bishops and priests.

Cardinal Ratzinger, who has read the Third Secret, confirms that it concerns the loss of faith and its consequences. What are the **consequences** of losing faith? **"Demonic confusion within Catholicism ... the loss of souls.... persecutions ... martyrdom of holy people...the breakdown of society - famine, wars, annihilation of nations... etc."**

As one loses his faith, he not only loses his faith, but embraces a "demonic faith" - he persecutes Christ's true disciples. Therefore, we have **apostasy within** the church - apostasy brought on by our own cardinals, bishops and priests.

The faithful are persecuted and are martyred - not only by those who should be "kept in bounds" by the Christian majority -- the "anti-God" factions of the world; but also, by "fallen away Catholics" (such as some Cardinals, bishops, priests, etc.) who remain within **THE ESTABLISHMENT CHURCH.**

Ideologies clash and the "anti-God" factions are prevailing. Truly Catholic order brings authentic individual peace as well as social peace and prosperity. The absence of such order and the imposition of an "anti-Catholic" or "anti-God" order brings with it the destruction of the social order as well as famines, wars and the annihilation of nations. God-rejecting systems are Satan's systems and Satan has come to confuse, seduce, incite conflicts, disrupt, distort, destroy and murder.

As Jesus stated, Satan is a LIAR and a MURDERER from his very beginning. Now, Satan has seated himself within the sanctuary of the Catholic Church (as Pope Paul VI observed) and is bringing about THE ABOMINATION OF DESOLATION.

Our only hope for peace is to consecrate Russia as God commands through Our Lady of Fatima. Then, we will enjoy God's order of true peace. "In the end My Immaculate Heart will triumph, the Holy Father will consecrate Russia to Me, Russia will be converted and a period of peace will be granted to mankind" - Our Lady of Fatima.

It will be late when the Pope obeys God and makes the proper collegial or ecclesial Fatima Consecration. It will be late, but it is never too late (on this side of death) to obey God and conform, by the help of His grace, to His will.

Demand A Divorce Or A Radical Annulment!

You have a right and an obligation to demand that the Vatican-Moscow marriage be declared null and void. Such a marriage clearly has a right to a radical annulment.

The Vatican-Moscow marriage is not valid from its beginning. The Vatican had no right to betray Christ for Russia. The "mega-forces" in the Church have absolutely no right to exchange Fatima for Moscow or Mary for the presently-reigning charismatic man-appointed world leader.

Any "children" born of the VATICAN-MOSCOW marriage are illegitimate and must be denounced as such. Glasnost and the consecration cover-up (claiming by lies that Russia was consecrated as Fatima demanded) must be exposed and denounced for being illegitimate.

How can this divorce and related denouncements come about? The Pope along with HIS higher clergy, by God's grace

38

and their graced cooperation, must see the "awe-ful" truth, admit their awful sins, confess them to God, make reparation and finally DO what God desires -- make the proper ecclesial awesome Fatima Consecration.

As it were, they, the hierarchy, must take back their God-given role. Borrowing the words of presently prevailing modernistic heresy: THEY ARE CHURCH. No longer is MAN, THE COMMUNITY, or the people-community, CHURCH.

In humility, the Pope along with HIS bishops and priests must come back to their true Bridegroom, CHRIST. They must renounce and radically divorce or annul their love affair with MAN -- the people, the communities, self-centered individuals, the man-acknowledged HEAD OF THE WORLD COMMUNITY, etc.

The Pope, along with HIS bishops, must come to obey God's will as given at Fatima. They must publicly acknowledge that RUSSIA --as a socio-political entity --is evil and therefore in need of consecration or dedication to God AND THAT RUSSIA'S ERRORS ARE GROSS SINS AGAINST GOD AND MANKIND AND MUST BE RENOUNCED AND CONDEMNED.

The Pope, along with HIS bishops, must become SINCERELY devoted to the Blessed Virgin Mary. Such devotion will be shown by their making THE AWESOME ECCLESIAL FATIMA CONSECRATION.

What can you do? At the very least, make your personal consecration to Mary. Then, promote, support and further the proper ecclesial consecration through the prudent and dedicated use of your time, money, prayers, etc.

The History Of Fatima: A History Of Cover-Ups

Our Lady came at Fatima for our **good.** She warned us about the only and uttermost present evil, SIN. She promised us that SIN would be punished -- now and in eternity; physically and spiritually;and, individually, ecclesially and socially.

She even gave Her favored children a vision of the utmost, ultimate and only eternal evil -- **Hell.** She reminded us of our great opportunity -- to console Jesus and Mary and to save and sanctify ourselves and others. YET, how have we reacted? **WE NOT ONLY DISOBEYED GOD, BUT WE ALSO TRIED TO JUSTIFY OUR AWFUL DISOBEDIENCE WITH COVER-UPS.**

Historically, one of the very first cover-ups of the Fatima Message was, what we could call, "natural." Fatima was considered to be a provincial or local happening without worldwide or "church-wide" significance.

Then, as a few of us began to perceive the "**awesome-ness**" of the Fatima Message, some of us "covered it up." Fatima was an embarrassment to modern man.

As we have seen, demonic forces operating through men are at work clouding over or covering up the **real Fatima Message** -- especially, in its ecclesial dimension. Even when a "window of opportunity" opened up in 1960 -- as Our Lady had predicted -- the Pope and bishops chose MAN and rejected God. Fatima was rejected. Man in the form of Russia was preferred.

Then came the Great Fall of 1989. Ecclesial authorities again preferred MAN (in the form of Russia) to God. THE GREAT FATIMA COVER-UP was issued and enforced.

Now (in 1991 and beyond), do we continue this great cover-up or do we -- in particular, the Pope and bishops -- see our horrible sins, confess, repent, call for reparation and properly consecrate Russia (thus, renouncing MAN as God or, in Our Lady of Fatima's words, "Russia's errors")?

The Fatima Message tests our basic allegiance. Is it to God or to MAN?

The Fatima Message must be rejected in those periods of history when Man is God -- when, in effect, MAN is worshipped in the place of God. In such periods of history, we are "blind to," cover-up, ignore or lie about the awesome truth -- the Fatima Message and our grossly sinful failure to obey God's commands as given to us at Fatima.

Indeed, history is repeating itself. In the forties, out of fear of offending Russia, we "covered-up" our gross failure to obey the Fatima Message. In the early sixties, out of fear of offending Russia, again, we "covered-up" our gross disobedience. In the nineties, out of fear of offending Russia, yet again, we "cover-up" our grossly sinful failure to comply with the real Fatima Message.

Why do we have "cover-ups?" The Fatima Message, to say the least, is AWESOME! Man, even in the midst of his "sin-caused-blindness," still realizes that he "can't" face the "aweful truths of Fatima" -- he must "cover-up" or lie about the Real Fatima Message and/or our disobedience to God's Fatima DEMANDS.

40

The Pope's Challenge Today

Our Lady told Sister Lucy that the Pope would have to **command** the bishops to join him in the ecclesial Fatima Consecration. Perhaps, he will have to command them under "pain of forced retirement" or even "under pain of excommunication."

Is the Pope ready to do this? Is the Pope "graced" to do this? Why **doesn't** he obey God?

It would **seem** that the Pope is looking at the world **naturally** and without the **vision of faith. Naturally,** there exists little or no possibility of successfully performing the ecclesial Fatima Consecration. The church seems to be hopelessly corrupt and filled with anarchy and dissension.

The Pope seems to be waiting for a divine intervention. But, does not God expect the "faith-filled" to "step out on faith?"

Here's **our ultimate answer.** It is given by Sister Lucy: "Pray for the Holy Father. Pray. Pray. Pray." Pray that the Pope may be given "effective graces" so that he will **do** what God demands at Fatima.

Pray and, as it were, win for the Pope the gift of **faith in action** - a faith that will lead him to be willing to join the martyrs of all ages. Pray for the Holy Father that he may come **to walk by faith** and not by sight. The Fatima Message assures us that when a sufficient number of us personally make and live **the awesome Fatima personal consecration -- then God will "grace" the Pope into obeying the Fatima Command.**

Live a life of prayer -- of uniting your mind, heart and deeds to God. Pray. Pray. Pray. Pray so that the Pope will come to walk by faith and not by sight.

Pray for the Pope. Pray that God may "grace him" to say "**NO**" **TO MAN AND "YES" TO GOD.**

Pray with a sense of urgency. Try to understand the awesome nature of the ecclesial Fatima Consecration. It's a matter of life or death - physically and spiritually, temporally and eternally, individually and communally; ecclesially and ecumenically (for the world).

Also, work for **God's** will to be done. "PUSH" for the proper ecclesial consecration. Do so with a sense of urgency.

Our Lord told Sister Lucy (August 1931): "They did not want to heed My request. Like the king of France they will **repent** but it will be LATE. Russia will have already spread her 'errors' throughout the world, causing wars and persecutions of the Church.

The Holy Father will have much to suffer."

Russia's Errors

Realize that Russia's **errors** will spread throughout the world. The U.S.A., as Alexander Solzhenitsyn observed, is "voluntarily" communistic and is becoming more and more so every day as we slide into ever increasing: socialism, official denial of God, suppression of free religious speech, government-control, etc. Russia's **errors** are influencing our lives more and more as time goes on.

Prayer and sacrifice (as well as properly applied "pressure," of course) will bring about the ecclesial Fatima Consecration. Then, as Russia is converted, we will be freed from Russia's errors as we return to our "God-given" American Constitution and "God-ly" living.

What is Russia's **main error?** The affirmation of Man as god and the denial of God (especially, as revealed in His one true Church). Therefore, Pope Pius XI in **Divini Redemptoris** boldly stated: "Communism is **intrinsically evil** and no one may collaborate with it in any undertaking whatever."

Russia's Errors Affect Our Church

The Catholic Church is in schism within itself. In North America, liberal apostates **control** much of the church.

Their "dictatorial dominance" is experienced in areas and projects such as: diocesan sacramental programs, RENEW, most indoctrinations for adults to become Catholics through RCIAs, "feely-touchy" liturgies and guidance sessions, doctrine-less and emotional catecheses, the removal of Christ from the central place in His churches, etc. The list goes on and on - as anyone with a modicum of knowledge about the contemporary church can attest.

The heart of our internal decadence is the same heart which accounts for "Russia's errors." Man is elevated above and/or in the place of God and God's Revealed Will for man. We no longer love God and man "for the sake of God." We love man for the sake of man - this is the heart of the RUSSIAN ERROR. This is also the heart of our APOSTASY WITHIN.

Two opposing forces exist within Catholicism. They exist within the Vatican itself. In fact, as in America, the "Man-affirming" mega-force seems to be in control of most of the Vatican. Many of the "upper clergy" perceive the PRESENT-

LY REIGNING RUSSIAN DICTATOR and the Pope as being of one mind -- they both agree that "man is central."

Is There Any Hope For The Future?

Is there any hope for the Church? Does the Third Secret tell us that cardinals, bishops and priests are falling into an eternal Hell like leaves off a tree? (If it doesn't, it should.)

We are in critical times. We are in the end-times. Jesus assured us that in the end-times deception would strengthen and multiply (Mt. 24:11).

What hope do **we** have? What hope do **you** have? Listen to Our Lady of Fatima. Do what She asks of **you.**

Pray, obey, mortify and convert (come to true faith and grow in it). In a special way, be devoted to praying the Rosary and be devoted to the Immaculate Heart of Mary -- in spirit and in truth.

Dedicate yourself to Mary. Consecrate yourself to Mary. In consecrating yourself to the only sinless human person, you consecrate yourself to your Lord and Saviour, Jesus.

These are the times foretold in the Apocalypse. Sister Lucy directed us to chapters eight through thirteen.

The Lady of Genesis who crushes Satan's head returns to be pursued by Satan (*Apoc. 12*). Yet, those who are under Her mantle will be protected by God from real harm (*Apoc. 12:15-17*).

Be consecrated to Our Lady of Fatima. Thus, you will be saved and you will profitably witness to others in these end-times by what you say and do and by your efforts to bring about the ecclesial consecration of Russia in accord with Fatima's **demands.**

Will **this** Pope obey God's Fatima Command for the proper ecclesial consecration of Russia? Perhaps. There are a **few** indications that things are changing towards accepting God's uncompromising will and doing as **He** desires.

Centesimus Annus (5/1/91), a papal encyclical, proclaimed a clear endorsement for **responsible** "capitalism" or for free and responsible enterprise and **against socialism as manifested in welfare states** (such as the U.S.A.).

Your abiding task is to **pray and work (orare et lab-orare)** so that God "may be led to" grace the Pope to do as He demanded at Fatima. In this book, you will come to see the absolute urgency of **YOUR** doing what you should.

You must be convinced of the mega-urgency of obeying the Fatima command. **You** must pray for God's graces to enable the

43

Pope to obey God. Also, **you** must do all you can to "pressure the Church, and Rome, in particular into" obeying God's Fatima Command.

You must pray and work so that the Pope (this one or the next one) will be a "**Pope of the impossible.**" Pray and work so that he will come to possess that fullness of faith which will lead him to join the great martyr-saints of Catholicism and embrace "**God's 'impossible' will.**"

God's "impossible" will is impossible for those who do not have the fullness of faith. God's "impossible" will is the "only possibility" for those who possess the fullness of faith.

Will History Repeat Itself?

Fatima -- as we have proven -- is **God's** prophecy to us in our day. **As such,** it must be believed in and acted upon.

On the natural plane we learn from prophetic history that prophecy **isn't** accepted most of the time. The period of Israel's classical prophets **proves** that **usually most** of "God's people" reject true prophecy and that only the remnant are saved. The majority must suffer God's wrath -- most often at the hands of their "god-less" and God-rejecting enemies.

When Will We Wake Up?

When will we realize that false ecumenism -- union with MAN as well as with those who worship MAN and not GOD, union with schismatic orthodox "Christians," union with heretical Protestants and the toleration of, as well as the promotion of, apostasy within -- are totally detestable to God? At Fatima, Mary insisted that mankind must stop offending God.

When will we once again perceive our horrible SINS? When will we wake up to the Reality of Sin as the only and ultimate evil? When will we repent, make reparation and make the Fatima consecrations? When will the gift of faith and a spirit of contrition and reparation for SIN lead us to make and to live the awesome Fatima consecrations?

At the very least, by God's grace and your graced cooperation, **YOU** can make and live the awesome **personal** Fatima consecration. **Then, you** will be led to work and pray so as to bring about the ecclesial Fatima consecration.

44

The Fatima Cover-up Is One Of Many Cover-Ups

Within the modern Church, "mega-cover-ups" abound. Why? The faithless and un-faithful (to God and His Church) higher clergy (and, especially their leaders) have disobeyed God and obeyed MAN. Furthermore, they abandon the truth about their sinfulness and embrace lies. They lie in order to "justify" or cover-up their sinfulness.

Cover-ups exist as we refuse to face the truth that we **have sinned** in our duty to witness to truth or in disobeying God. There are at least two other (less significant?) Fatima cover-ups; as well as, **many** other ecclesial cover-ups.

Yet, the proper Fatima consecrations will act "sacramentally" -- to bring sinners back to truth and to a firm resolution to abandon (and expose) sinful cover-ups. Making and living the Fatima consecrations will bring us **GOD'S GRACE AND MERCY.**

A Human Fatima "Cover-Up?"

Is Sister Lucy "the human Fatima cover-up?" Up to the **FALL** of 1989, Sister Lucy was as accessible to the public as any other world-renowned public figure would be in her circumstances. Then, after the enforcement of the consecration cover-up, Sister Lucy seems to have become "the human Fatima cover-up."

Since the **FALL** of 1989, we can only "communicate with" Sister by going through her bishop and then speaking to her **through** her superioress. Furthermore, this "screened, censored and totally controlled" communication when it is given, is usually given only to those who strictly adhere to **THE PARTY LIE.**

Since the **FALL** of 1989, Sister is no longer allowed to **freely and clearly** express the truth about the heinous evils involved with suppressing and distorting the Fatima Messages and Commands, especially as regards the existence of the Fatima Consecration Cover-up. Before this **FALL,** she clearly and unhesitatingly professed on at least five different occassions that the 1984 papal consecration **did not fulfil God's command as given at Fatima.**

Another Fatima Cover-Up: Watering-Down The Fatima Challenge

The Fatima demand for proper consecrations is, at times,

treated in a shallow and superficial way. Consecration for the great mass of shallow and superficial "Catholics" does not include a consecrated LIFE and REAL REPARATION -- that's too much of a challenge. A sweet little "I love you" will suffice.

However, Fatima **demands** reparation - daily prayers and sufferings for sinners (oneself and others) out of love for Jesus and Mary who are offended by sins and for sinners who suffer the effects of sin.

On Friday, July 13, 1917, Our Lady disclosed the great secret, part of which stated: "...I shall come to ask for the consecration of Russia to My Immaculate Heart **and** the Communion of Reparation on the First Saturdays [of each month, preceded by Confession and accompanied by fifteen minutes of meditation on the 15 Mysteries of the Rosary]."

Ruling forces within the establishment-church desire to please MAN. They will not tolerate the **awful and awesome** Fatima Message. Was not Fr. Fuentes a victim of such forces?

Fr. Fuentes in 1957 disclosed that Sr. Lucy assured him that **many** nations **will be** destroyed and, worse yet, that **MANY** were going to Hell for ignoring the Fatima Message. After that, he was removed from one of his positions.

Don't cover-up Fatima's deep challenge by reducing consecration to a shallow, superficial, sanctimonious and sweet "I like Mary and Jesus." The Fatima consecrations are so AWESOME that they determine the temporal and eternal mode of being not only of yourself but of others as well. The Fatima consecrations are so AWESOME that they determine the fate of the Roman Catholic Church and THUS of the entire world. Don't trivialize and **trash** these AWESOME FATIMA CONSECRATIONS.

Indeed, real reparation and an awesome "living" consecration are God's commands. They are given to us at Fatima - as well as throughout HIS WORD TO US, the Holy Bible.

The "Third Secret" Cover-Up
And The Fatima Cover-Up

There also exists the cover-up of the Third Secret (at least, through November of 1991). The Third Secret of Fatima has not been MADE PUBLIC as Our Lady requested on Jan. 2, 1944. At the latest, it was supposed to have been MADE PUBLIC in 1960.

To justify this **failure to obey**, we are treated to a "jumble" of contradictory lies. These lies are encapsulated in two contradictory statements.

"The secret is not for our times - it does not concern us." **AND** "The secret pertains to the loss of faith (and thus the loss of souls) and/or terrible punishments (such as, the enslavement of the world by atheistic communism or the New Age)."

Obviously - to anyone with a modicum of intelligence and right thinking - a **clumsy** COVER-UP of the truth has been employed. God help those who are wicked enough to go along with such "party-lines" and betray Jesus with a "Judas KISS."

Not only are there "direct" Fatima cover-ups, but also other cover-ups of our sins in disobeying and betraying God.

Un-faithful (to God and to His Church) and faith-less higher clergy and those who rule such clergy are "naturally led" (by demonic forces) to justify their grave sins of passively or actively condoning doctrinal and moral evils of the highest magnitude such as: abortion, homosexuality, socialism, those types of annulments which are de facto divorces by another name; liturgical and catechetical abuses which lead one not only to deny Catholic Dogma; but also, at times, to embrace the post-Christian and neo-pagan tenets of New Age "Catholicism."

In an age filled with demonically originating cover-ups within the very sanctuary of God's One and Only True Church, we emphasize the Fatima Consecrations as the expression of our commitment to truth and as the "sacramental source" of our being liberated from the powers of darkness - the abomination of desolation, where the Evil One is being more and more enthroned in the very sanctuary of God's One, Holy, Universal and Apostolic Roman Catholic Church.

The Cover-Up: A Mega-Sin And A "Dogma"

The Fatima Consecration cover-up is a horrible sin -- a "mega-sin." It comes from a "mega-rejection" of God's will. It surpasses Adam and Eve's "cover-ups" in duration as well as in "intensity." Not only does it cover-up the truth, "justify" its disobedience -- but, in Satanic Pride, it is now trying to "dogmatize" such a cover-up.

We -- the non-experts and the non-official-authorities -- must believe what official authorities and their selected experts

"dogmatically decree." We are commanded to abandon God and our common sense in order to embrace the ABOMINATION OF DESOLATION -- MAN, enthroned as God, within GOD'S SANCTUARY, THE ROMAN CATHOLIC CHURCH.

Indeed, the Fatima cover-up is a "mega-cover-up." As such, it concerns and determines the temporal and eternal fate of human beings. As such, it breeds other cover-ups. As a "mega-sin," it breeds and/or expresses other sins.

For example, a false ecumenism accounts for and comes from the consecration cover-up. This false ecumenism leads us to hold that the Russian Orthodox Church -- which is both a puppet of atheistic communism and schismatic -- is fully and truly Christian in the eyes of God and Mary.

Nothing could be further from the truth. Such "bishops" are either officers in the KGB or directly controlled by KGB officers.

As the Russian Orthodox Church is allowed to expand, we should not be duped into thinking that Russia is being converted. However, if one believes the cover-up, then one tends to believe that Russia is being converted as the Russian Orthodox Church expands.

Also, the Fatima consecration cover-up is a mega-sin because it breeds apostasy within. Our morals, our liturgy and our dogma-related catechesis continually become more and more corrupt. They will worsen until we make our consecrations -- in spirit and in truth.

For example, a liberal (faithless and unfaithful) type of superficial and moral or imagined unity of bishops with the Pope is not only presumed to have existed at the time of the 1984 consecration of this world to the Immaculate Heart of Mary, but we are also commanded by the apostates within to protect and to promote such "unity."

However, Our Lady specified that "the Pope in union with the Catholic bishops of the world" was to consecrate Russia. This unity must be real, not imagined or politically contrived.

True unity does not come into being by the "fiat" of those who oppose and reject the real Fatima Message. True unity does not come into being by the creation of a nice "theological rule" -- **that as the Pope acts so do all the bishops.** The Pope when he "officially" acts, acts collegially -- therefore all the bishops join him in every official deed.

God does not play such "wishful" theological games. The Catholic bishops of the world must freely be -- or "forced" to be -- actually united with the Pope in making, as they themsel-

48

ves individually make, the prescribed Fatima consecration of Russia on the same day as the Pope makes it.

In the name of this false "wishful" unity (which is totally alien to the present state of **disunity** of the Pope with all of the Catholic bishops), we are also urged and commanded "**ex cathedra**" to cease and desist from stating the obvious: Russia was **not** consecrated in 1984 as Our Lady requested.

Indeed, not only did the Pope lack true collegiality in such a consecration, he also failed to consecrate **Russia** -- Russia is Russia; the world is the world.

In the name of a **false, sinful** and **imagined** unity we are ordered to hold and propagate the "party line." We are urged to lie in order to "cover-up" the **sinful** disobedience of our higher clergy. [Even the title of the 1984 Consecration declares the truth. This consecration was entitled: "THE CONSECRATION OF **THE WORLD** TO THE IMMACULATE HEART OF MARY." **Russia** was not the object of the 1984 consecration.]

At present, **true unity** can only be attained and expressed as the Pope **demands** (under "pain" of forced retirement or excommunication) that every Catholic bishop actually join him in word and in deed on a specific day in consecrating RUSSIA (**not** the world) **as God commanded** and as Mary desired.

In the name of "unity," the alleged "Fatima-ists" who are really against Fatima also elevate the party-line -- **that Russia has been consecrated in 1984 as Mary desired** -- to the status of a **dogma** of the church (even as they ignore or reject true Catholic dogmas).

Indeed these apostates are the worst of sinners. They not only are destroying God's church from within, but they are also trying to destroy God's church "in the name of God" as they try to convince their unwary victims (God's sheep) that God Himself in THE Fatima Message concurs with or agrees with their lies.

Chapter Four

The "Ultimate" Choice -- Consecrations Or The New Age Dictatorship And Ever-Worsening Destruction

First of all, consecrate yourself to the Immaculate Heart of Mary. Then, pray, sacrifice and work so as to bring about the ecclesial Fatima consecration of Russia. Also, spread or promulgate the real, full and authentic Fatima Message.

WHY? Less than TWO PERCENT of American "Catholics" have even a modicum of understanding concerning the Fatima Message. Furthermore, less that ONE PERCENT have an authentic and undistorted understanding of THE POST-BIBLICAL PROPHECY -- the word of God as given to us at Fatima.

Until you and others (in a sufficient number) receive and obey the Fatima Message, you and others will continue to be enslaved to Russia's errors and eventually to a new "mega-Russia" or to the New Age world religion and world dictatorship -- an indescribable horror of men dominated by men and thus by Satan (cf. Rv. 13).

By God's grace and your graced cooperation, you will come to perceive that the Fatima consecrations are indeed not only "most awesome;" but also, "most urgent." Our continuing disobedience is bringing about our worsening punishments.

The Prime End-Times Sacramental

A sacramental (as well as a Sacrament) is designated by God to have two concurrent dynamic moments. Each God-defined or God-chosen sacramental can: (1) bring God to man; (2) bring man to God.

THE PRIME (GOD-CHOSEN) END-TIMES SACRAMENTAL IS THE IMMACULATE HEART OF MARY. Through our real devotion and consecration to Mary, God will come to us to save us and we will be able to go to God -- so as to attain and retain not only salvation and sanctification, but also graces far beyond (and yet, within) these most precious gifts (for ourselves and for others).

True devotion to Mary is CONSECRATION TO HER IM-MACULATE HEART. Consecration to Mary's Immaculate Heart will bring us to desire, think and live as Mary. We will become Mary's special children -- in spirit and in truth.

True devotion to Mary demands that we OBEY THE FATIMA MESSAGE. It demands our awesome consecrations -- both personal and ecclesial. At present, we will consider the ecclesial consecration (in part three, we will consider this consecration in greater detail).

As the Pope with HIS bishops DO what God demands at Fatima -- they will embrace the prime end-times sacramental. God's graces will be poured out upon Russia, upon God's Church and upon individuals throughout the entire world. These blessings will be both temporal and eternal; both to the Church and to the world; both to individuals and to nations; and, both physical and spiritual.

Individuals will then be led to God's true Church -- the Catholic Church. Russia -- as a social and political entity -- will renounce its most horrible sins and sinful system and be converted to Catholicism. Also, God's Church will be restored to its pristine and proper purity and glory.

We are assured by God of these as well as others blessings. Why? God Himself spoke to us at Fatima (as was proven in the first chapter).

As usual, hope comes from faith. We who believe God, believe the Fatima Message. We have hope. We live with hope. We look forward to that day when the Pope will obey God and embrace devotion to Mary as God demands. We realize that the Fatima Consecrations are AWESOME.

An Emerging New Age Power

There are only two mega-powers in our world. They are Russia and the Vatican. These two powers control or greatly influence most of the world. The "Moslem force" is "fractionalized" and not universal.

The Fatima Messages presumed this fact at a time when it was very far from being a fact. As the political and social entity, Russia goes, so goes the world.

At present, Russia's errors are spreading throughout the world (especially, in the Americas) -- this is exactly as Our Lady of Fatima predicted. Also, Russia's military might is the most powerful that the world has ever witnessed. Both Russia's political and military activity extend to **most** of the world.

Yet, the other mega-power, the Vatican (and especially, the Pope) is infinitely stronger than Russia. Whenever, the Pope, as it were, activates the Prime End-times Sacramental, he will defeat the evil empire of Russia as a political, social and religious entity. Thus, he will bring peace to this world.

At present, however, the evil empire is expanding. It's "wounding" is only temporary. The Beast will **marvelously recover.** The rest of the world will admire and be amazed at the Beast's recovery (Rev. 13:3).

Let's see how the Beast, the evil empire, is doing at the present time. How is it becoming the New Age Monster predicted by Our Lady of Fatima?

New Age leader, Fritj Cupra (**The Turning Point**) is quoted in a New Age newsletter on politics (6/25/90) as claiming that Russia's "new thinking" agrees with New Age goals. **Time** (6/18/90) quoted Gorbachev: "All mankind is entering a new age, and world trends are beginning to obey new laws and logic."

Ivan Frolov, a master-mind of New Age Humanism was named editor of the Soviet Union's most powerful newspaper, **Pravda** in 1990. His outlook is described in his book (**Man-Science-Humanism**): "We deplore efforts to denigrate human intelligence... seeking to explain the world in supernatural terms, and to look outside of nature for salvation."

The New Age Religion affirms Man as God and **rejects** GOD. Is this the abomination of desolation? Certainly, this is the curse we have brought -- and **are** bringing -- on ourselves and others by our not making and living the AWESOME FATIMA CONSECRATIONS.

New Age Catholicism

A major part of the New Age Dictatorial Enslavement is the gradual imposition of this New Age Religion. In place of the One True Religion from God (the Catholic Religion) we have **many** paths to Human Fulfillment. In place of Catholicism we have **a** general watered down "Christian" movement. In place of a general Christian movement, we have a **Man-is-God** movement.

Is not New Age "**Catholicism**" actually here? Is it not an "established practice?" **De facto,** no longer is the Pope considered to be the Head of the Church and **the** Vicar of Christ on earth. He is, according to many, the first of bishops, at best, and one of the bishops, "at worst."

Actually, most "Catholics" in the "Euro-American" churches do not believe that the Pope's will is God's will. It's **an** opinion. (More that three-fourths of American "Catholic" youth **reject** papal infallibility. **Most** American "Catholics" prefer only a symbolic union with Rome).

In practice, the Pope is **not** free to impose his will in the church. As the three seers of Fatima perceived in a vision, the Pope is a prisoner of the controlling prelates within the Vatican, even as he is being attacked from "outside."

In practice, the church is no longer Catholic and One -- universally united in doctrine and (moral and liturgical) practice. Each national or regional church increasingly determines Catholicism for its people and according to the desires of MAN -- the experts and/or the people. (**Most** American "Catholics" disagree with one or more **essential** Catholic teachings.)

In practice, the Catholic Church is no longer APOSTOLIC -- holding onto full **Biblical** Truth (God's Revealed Will). It has perverted not only the Bible's teachings, but the very words of the Bible. **In practice, GOD'S WORD becomes MAN'S WORD** (as we cater to the feelings of the heretics-within as well as the feelings of various factions, such as the feminists).

For example, our "revered scripture experts" -- probably to reduce or destroy Jesus' image -- render Mary's "I do not know a man (Lk.1:34)." **into:** "I do not have a husband." You know what that "makes Jesus become."

Also, for example, some of our worshipped experts assure us that we can earn salvation as they transform an "impossible-to-pay" debt of ten thousand talents (in Mt. 18:24 -- a debt equivalent to trillions of dollars) into a payable "huge amount."

A final example reflects and approves of our total spiritual depravity and faithlessness regarding marriage: "Let the marriage bed be undefiled (Hb. 13:4)" is conveniently changed into God's blanket endorsement of whatever happens on the marriage bed (after all, **sex** is GOD). Check your "Bible" for these and other aberrations or defilements of God's Holy Word.

Try, if you can, to comprehend the horrendous extent of our pride. We have allowed and even "appointed" THE REVERED AND SELF-PROCLAIMED EXPERTS to decide what God SHOULD HAVE SAID! The discovery of the Dead Sea Scrolls proved that the Bible -- **GOD'S** Word -- did not suffer **any** significant change in transmission over a period of well over two thousand years (up to 1940 within the Catholic Church). Yet, from 1940 to the present -- the Bible itself has suffered **many**

54

significant changes at the hands of our evil-minded "experts" as they continually give us "newer and more improved" **versions** (at least, the're honest and don't claim that their distortions are **translations**) of God's Word.

In practice, therefore, the Catholic Church (except for the faithful and "faith-filled" remnant) is already in certain crucial areas the NEW AGE CATHOLIC CHURCH. At the very least, we are RIPE FOR THE NEW AGE. The only hope for the future is that our leaders be given and act on God's grace to totally renounce their present direction. HOW? By making that AWESOME ECCLESIAL FATIMA CONSECRATION (ALONG WITH, OF COURSE, THEIR OWN PERSONAL ACTS OF CONSECRATION TO MARY).

The proper ecclesial consecration -- according to the **true** Fatima Message -- will bring about not only a halt to the Church's (and **thus** the world's) descent into Satan's Kingdom on Earth -- but also a reversal of direction. This reversal will be so awesome that not only Catholicism in practice will return to true Catholicism; but also, **Russia** will become truly Catholic.

Therefore, obey Mary. Pray for the Pope. Pray that he may come to embrace the **prime end-times sacramental**. Pray that he may be graced to obey God and **to make the proper awesome ecclesial consecration of Russia to the Immaculate Heart of Mary.**

Russia's Conversion -- The Awesome Fruit Of Obeying God

"If My requests are heeded, Russia will be converted ..." As I write these words, **many** within the church contend that we have fulfilled Our Lady's requests. They **assure** us that Russia is converting.

Even as we are continually immersed in gross social evils and in internal apostasy -- we are assured that all is well. Our Lady's requests were complied with. Let's enjoy peace and safety even admidst wars, persecutions, famines and other tribulations.

Pray that you may retain your sanity and ability to think correctly in a church and society operating from and within (what the Real Sister Lucy described as) **"diabolic disorientation."** See the **"contradictions preached as truth"** by **apparently good** but actually **evil** Fatima "devotees."

When Russia -- AS A POLITICAL AND SOCIAL ENTITY

-- is **CONVERTED** to Catholicism (the only true religion) -- then, we know for sure that Fatima's requests have been heeded. Russia's conversion will be the fruit of our awesome Fatima consecrations -- personal and ecclesial. Russia is Russia, AND conversion is conversion to Catholicism -- don't let anyone confuse you concerning such basic self-evident truths.

In this age of false ecumenism, we must remind ourselves that God, Our Lord and Mary define "conversion" as coming to the one and only true church of Jesus Christ -- the Roman Catholic Church. Nothing short of that can be considered to be conversion. Therefore, the conversion of Russia is its conversion to the Roman Catholic Church -- **not** to "Christianity."

The ultimate choice concerns ultimate end-time reality. Either Russia (and thus most of the world) will be Catholic (in the true and full sense of the word) OR Russia (and thus most of the world) will be New Age (religiously and politically) and much of the world will be destroyed. This is the FATIMA MESSAGE. Indeed, it is AWESOME -- it concerns the future of our world. The Fatima Challenge is also AWESOME -- make the Fatima consecrations or ....

Chapter Five

A Very Brief History Of The Church As It Refers To The Personal Fatima Consecration

Remember the years from 1917-1960. They were years of strong Catholicism in North America. Seminaries were being expanded. The future was bright. Why?

At that time, the present was filled with (what Malachi Martin calls) CATHOLIC INTIMACY. We spoke of and "prayed" devotion and consecration to Jesus and to Mary. Consequently, we lived consecrated lives.

NOW, however, we live in the midst of "CATHOLIC COLDNESS" AND INTERNAL APOSTASY. WHAT WAS A MAJOR TURNING POINT?

Pope John the Twenty-third refused to make public the Third Secret and refused to make the ecclesial consecration of Russia (as the bishops came to Rome for the Second Vatican Council). Through one Pope (as well as previous and subsequent ones), God's special graces were withdrawn from "Western Catholicism." Likewise, through the faith, hope and love of one Pope, even now, each of us once again (as in the times of CATHOLIC INTIMACY AND FLOURISHING DOCTRINAL UNITY) could be blessed with God's special graces.

Your personal consecration becomes more difficult within a church which ignores and even "blasphemes" the real Lady of Fatima. It would be "quite easy" to obey God's Fatima Demands if we dwelt within an atmosphere of CATHOLIC INTIMACY AND FLOURISHING DOCTRINAL UNITY.

Instead, we live within an atmosphere of CATHOLIC COLD-NESS and INTERNAL APOSTASY. Why? Ultimately, because the Popes have disobeyed God - they have failed in faith, hope and love.

God's Providence often relies on one man - our hierarchical representative and God's representative to us (the Vicar of Christ on earth). God's Providence throughout history often has relied on one man (or woman) - Mary, Adam, Abraham, Moses, etc.

Yet, God also "relies on" each of us. Personal consecration is possible and more urgent than ever before. In fact -- according to Our Lady of Fatima -- if a sufficient number of IN-DIVIDUALS actually live consecrated lives, then the Pope will be "graced enough" to make the proper ecclesial Fatima Consecration.

As you read and pray this book, realize that you live not only under the "Adamic curse" but also under the curses of "past disobediences" -- especially those of the previous Popes and other religious, family and social leaders.

Let these "negative realities" lead you to be "positive." Forgive these past and present sinners -- don't hate them since in hating them you join them in SIN.

Instead, by grace, actualize the positive and actualize your individual potential. Realize that you are a unique individual of infinite "SELF-DETERMINING" dignity. Your individual dignity comes from your own RESPONSES TO GOD.

As YOU live "before God," determines YOUR OWN eternal existence - in Heaven or in Hell. Thus, you are "SELF-DETERMINING" your own infinite dignity or worth. (It is difficult to hold onto these and other basic truths within a Church and society which trivialize and trash the true dignity and worth of INDIVIDUALS -- even as they preach, promulgate, impose, "liturgy-tize" and dogmatize their LIES AND HERESIES.)

Accentuate the "positive." Live in Truth. As far as possible, live convinced that YOU are of infinite individual and unique responsibility and THUS, by your proper responses to God, of great eternal and unique dignity.

YOU must live a consecrated life, OR YOU will go to HELL. YOU must live a life that is consecrated to Mary and thus to Jesus or that is consecrated to Jesus through Mary.

The personal Fatima Consecration is AWESOME. It reaffirms the basic truths of real Catholicism which are denied by many Catholics. As you read and pray this book, seek God's graces to be FATIMA CONSECRATED -- in YOUR INDIVIDUAL desires, thoughts, words and deeds.

PART TWO

THE AWESOME FATIMA
PERSONAL CONSECRATION

Introduction to Part Two

This part of the book concerns **your** special Fatima Challenge. Here and in part four, you will come to a greater understanding and appreciation of "your personal consecration" -- its meaning and necessity. Then, **do** as God directs you.

Most likely, God will lead you to make or renew (on a regular basis) some type of **Fatima Personal Consecration Prayer** (three such prayers are presented in part four -- a daily, weekly and general one).

God will act in your life in order to lead you not only to make a personal consecration prayer; but also, to live the **AWESOME FATIMA PERSONAL CONSECRATION.** You will be led to live the consecration for God's glory, for the consolation of the Sacred Heart of Jesus and the Immaculate Heart of Mary and for the salvation and sanctification of yourself and others.

Chapter Six
Your Spiritual Milieu

You live within a "spiritual sewer" which is festering into ever more intense and increasing corruption. The chances are -- if you live in North America or the corrupt "West" -- that your society and church are on the brink of disaster.

God's mercy is being exhausted. He cannot help but purify and/or discard (or destroy) churches that have lost their flavor. THIS is God's Fatima Message and God's Biblical Message (cf. the Old Testament Prophets as well as Mk. 9:50; Apoc. 2;3).

However, in spite of establishment-sponsored propaganda -- you are an **individual.** The "COMMUNITY" is **not** YOU. The "community's" condition or destiny is not necessarily yours.

You can separate yourself (by God's grace and your graced cooperation) from the rotten community (II Cor. 6:17). **You can determine, by God's grace, your own individual life -- both here and forever and ever.**

In these end-times (which are described in the following scriptures: II Cor. 11:13; Acts 20:28-31; Pt. 3:3-9; I Tm. 4:14; II Tm. 3:1-5; II Thes. 2:9-12; Apoc. 8-13), seek out and find a priest who (as best **you** can judge) says a **valid** Mass (**he** intends to do what the church intends and does **not** have a totally contrary or invalidating intention). Likewise, seek out and find a "**valid** minister" of Baptism for your child. **Otherwise**, the Mass isn't a Mass and the Baptism isn't a Baptism.

Then, if possible, find (or "create") an orthodox or truly Catholic spiritual milieu for yourself and "your loved ones." Refuse to become a victim or comrade of any rotten community -- the world or the "worldy church."

In these end-times, there exists a special urgency for you to consecrate yourself to Mary and thus to Jesus or to Jesus through Mary. This is God's command. This is the **Awesome** Fatima Message, Challenge and Command.

Enemies Within

In order to (continually) realize the magnitude and extent of the urgency that is involved in your making the Fatima Personal Consecration, you need to become convinced of Reality. You now dwell among four types of "Catholics" who are really **your enemies within "Catholicism."** These four types are described below:

61

1. Catholics who are content to live on a superficial -- "**feely-touchy**"-- level. They are no longer Catholics since they have abandonded or will shortly abandon the "spirit and truth" or substance of **authentic** Catholicism. Unfortunately, a sizeable number of such "Catholics" can be found within the ranks of our clergy; and, especially, within the ranks of our "non-clerical" establishment leadership.

To **prove** this, all you need to do is to become familiar with the indoctrination techniques, teaching philosophy, goals and methods of currently imposed prayers, programs, policies and propaganda. More specificly, familiarize yourself with **Renew**; Enneagram Retreats; most versions of **R.C.I.A.**; many, if not most, sacramental preparation programs (for Baptism, First Communion, First Confession and Marriage); Clergy Continuing Education Sessions, the present **Novus Ordo** Mass prayers, ordinary preaching, "Catholic" catechesis and formation, etc. All of these too often endanger or even "steal away" your God-given truly Catholic faith (instead of imparting the true faith and fortifying it).

2. The next class of people originates from those who were victimized by the current internal apostasy. They were the "naive" people -- especially, our young people (e.g. through actual catechesis, and, in a special way, current sex indoctrination).

Pray for the unwary and the naive. Protect them from scandal and unnecessary temptations. Instruct them in truth. Witness to the truth by what you say and by what you do.

Remember that the "naive turned rotten" become the followers and supporters of the **enemies within.** Then, they become the **enemies within** -- by default and/or by "semi-deliberate positive cooperation."

3. The third type of "Catholics" who constitute the **enemies within** is composed of those who **willingly** join the side of evil -- for personal gain, for acceptance, for promotion, for power, to please the "gang," for money, etc. They want to be with the winners. They are "very dangerous."

These "Judases" abound within the church in North America. However, they are not only found among the clergy, but also among the ecclesial bureaucrats -- from heads of diocesan offices to parish "CCD" teachers.

4. The last type of "Catholics" who join the **enemies within** are those who **live in HATE** towards orthodox Catholics who dare to

disagree with them on "un-essentials." For these enemies within, the inessential is essential. Why? So they can live in hate of those who are truly Catholic.

Satan is their FATHER IN HATE. As they hate "for the sake of righteousness" -- they enter Satan's domain.

These enemies within cling to one or more "accidentals" or distortions of Catholicism and then raise them to the level of "essentials." Their sinful allegiance may be to an alleged seer, or it may be to an "elite-defining-charism" (such as speaking in tongues), or it may be to a custom, or it may be to a devotion to a false and imagined Mary, or it may be to the latest liturgical or catechetical un-Catholic or liberal decree from "the local establishment."

It is extremely unfortunate that such **HATE GROUPS** even cause divisions among those who should be addressing, attacking and removing **essential** evils within the church establishment. Let's stop sinning by **hating.** Let's stop our "inside fighting" while the modernist heretics are attacking and destroying most of the **essentials** of Catholicism.

We need to live convinced of essential truths. We need to defend these truths and to relentlessly attack those who are intent on destroying the Catholic Church from **within.**

In essentials, unity. In non-essentials, freedom. In everything, charity, especially in the primary and essential sense of the word -- OBEDIENCE to God and God's revealed will (e.g. God's Fatima Commands).

All of the above-mentioned types of **apostates** constitute or "define" the spiritual "rottenness" within which **you** are challenged to live. Separate from these apostates (when possible and/or when "for the best"). Oppose them. Try to convert them to the truth. Protect the "naive" or innocent from them.

Preserve and strengthen your faith. How? By being -- in spirit and in truth -- **consecrated to the Immaculate Heart of Mary and thus to the Sacred Heart of Jesus.**

Should You Confront The Enemies Within?

If and when you are consecrated to the Immaculate Heart of Mary and **thus** to the Sacred Heart of Jesus, you will not only be consecrated "in" Truth, you will be consecrated "to" Truth. You will be consecrated **to** Truth - you will live so that "God's will be done on earth."

How will you relate to the enemies within - to laymen, priests, bishops and even, perhaps, the Pope? You will **rebuke them** when the true faith is endangered or, worse yet, when it is being destroyed by them.

Why? You are obliged to do so. St. Thomas Acquinas, THE Catholic Theologian, stated: "if the faith were **endangered,** a subject **must** rebuke his prelate, even publicly **(Summa Theologica,** II-II, 33)."

There you have it! You are obliged under **"pain of sin"** to **rebuke** any and all prelates when the true Catholic faith is even **endangered.** Your obligation TODAY is "most serious." TODAY, we live in a church which suffers APOSTASY (or HERESY) **WITHIN.**

Also, you will be obedient to the Fatima Commands. You will offer prayers and sacrifices for the Holy Father and for all bishops and priests. As you do so, you will be led to urge them -- as taking the place of Christ and as "representing" yourself and others -- to be faithful to Christ and to act for the true well-being and prosperity of yourself and others.

Chapter Seven

Can You See The Truth?
Do You See What I See?

Quite a number of contemporary "Catholics" would perceive what is written in this book -- concerning the essential message, truths and commands of Fatima -- as being nonsense or threatening. As nonsense, they ignore Fatima. As threatening, they oppose the full Fatima message, truths and commands. **WHY** would they ignore or oppose the truth?

They have become damned by God to be as they are - to see evil as good, to see their pet errors as truth and to be dedicated to fighting what is good and true in the name of what they perceive to be good and true.

They **are under the "Romans One Curse." Read Romans chapter one, verse 14 to chapter two, verse 4.**

When anyone rejects God in his heart -- when he rejects the Truth in the depths of his being -- God delivers him to damnation. He becomes DAMNED BY GOD.

Rest assured that you are not one of these if you are truly consecrated to the Immaculate Heart of Mary, or even if are still able to doubt your demonic certitudes and question your demonic beliefs. God's graces are at work in those who doubt and question Satan's LIES.

Maybe, you have come close to being one sicf these - the DAMNED BY GOD. Thank God for letting you see the truth that will set you free. Then, be consecrated and thus be freed from confusion, doubt, despair, etc.

Consecrate yourself to truth. Be consecrated to truth. **This** was Jesus' solemn prayer for His disciples at the Last Supper (Jn. 17:17-20). **"Consecrate them in truth..."**

Your **consecration to the Immaculate Heart of Mary** -- giving yourself to God, to Truth, to obeying God with or by the grace and mercy of Christ given through Mary -- will bring you **to** and keep you **in** the Truth and in the true faith. You will be freed from the confusion, doubt, rationalizing and despair which leads one to being under the "Romans One Curse."

Pray. Pray. Pray. Pray for yourself - a sinner in danger of falling under the "Romans One Curse." Pray, sacrifice, obey and come to believe in (and to ever more fully believe in) through the intercession of Mary to Her Son, Jesus, Who lived and died for you to extend to you His **mercy and grace** (the message of the "Trinitarian-Crucifixion" Vision of Sister Lucy).

Let faith set you free. Faith makes evident the unseen world - Hb. 11:1. See the Truth. Come to live in Truth. No more will you live uncertain and confused about the essentials of life. You will be freed from the spirit of darkness, deception, confusion, hopelessness, terrifying fear, uncertainty, despair, etc.

If you are **not** confused, doubtful, self-justifying and the like -- thank God and thank Mary. **You** are under a special blessing in this age of diabolic delusions and confusions which are so strong as to become certitudes in the minds and hearts of **many** evil people.

Show your thanksgiving by consecrating yourself to Mary and thus to Jesus, the Truth. In doing this you dedicate yourself to perceiving and living the Truth -- not by your power but by the graces given you by Christ through the Immaculate Heart of Mary.

The Satanic Confirmed

Sister Lucy, the Seer of our times, stated the following: "Our times are VERY EVIL and we are WEAK - be attentive and diligent in obtaining strength from God...a diabolic disorientation invades us and misleads souls...it is painful to see such a great disorientation in so many who occupy places of responsibility... it is sad to see so many people letting themselves be dominated by the DIABOLIC WAVE sweeping across the world and that they are blinded to the point of being incapable of seeing error."

Padre Pio, the stigmatist of our times, wrote: "As long as the soul is not entirely purified, the LIGHT is night, darkness, fire and torture, but when ready to receive the Kiss of perfect union [or consecration], one becomes illumined by the LIGHT."

Consecrate yourself to the Immaculate Heart of Mary to be preserved from this wicked and perverse society and church. Be transformed into Christ for as Padre Pio stated: "Every predestined soul **must** resemble Jesus."

Those who resemble Jesus are not only consecrated to truth but also embrace the divine paradox of Fatima - the paradox of Christ's gospels or the paradox of the cross. Jesus and Mary lived this paradox fully and perfectly.

The Divine Paradox

The divine paradox is that to save your life, you must lose it. To be consecrated to Truth, you will need to **die** to your flesh (**your** brain and body) and to the world (the communities of men with their natural values).

It's that simple. It's that awesome and challenging. What is **your** answer? Are you willing to die in order to live?

"If a man will save his life, he must lose it (Lk. 17:33)... Unless the grain of wheat fall in the earth and die, it remains just a grain of wheat (Jn. 12:24)... What does it profit a man to gain the whole world and suffer the loss of his own soul?" (Mt. 16:26)

As you advance and "make great progress" in living your consecration to Mary, the divine paradox will become logical and "self-evidently" desirable. God through Mary will totally grace you or fully empower you to embrace the divine paradox of living, not you, but Christ in you (Gal. 2:20).

Chapter Eight
Consecrator, Covenant and Consecration

Christ is the Consecrator. His very being states this. His perfect human nature unites to the divine nature in the Second Person of the Blessed Trinity. It is only those who live in Christ who will be consecrated to God forever - Jesus is the One and Only Consecrator. He **alone** can be your Savior from eternal Hell.

Only as united with Him forever, will you be able to praise God and to live the very life of God (in as much as you are able to do so by God's power). Separated from God forever, you will dwell in eternal Hell. The choice is an individual choice. The choice is **yours.**

Yet, salvation is God's gift. This gift is offered in Christ. This gift is offered in the Covenant "of" and "in" Christ. Each is free. Each is free to accept or reject Covenant through consecration. God's grace and our free will "define" the mystery of salvation as "contained in" God's covenant and our consecration.

But, first of all, especially in our post-Christian and pre-pagan meta-physical atmosphere, we need to emphasize and become convinced of our "FALLEN-NESS" We need salvation. We can't save ourselves. We need the Consecrator -- Jesus, God and Saviour.

The Fallen Need Consecration

Hardly had sacred Adam issued from the hand of God when he, our prime hierachical representative, decided to de-sacralize himself and those whom he represented -- us.

Ever since then, each human person (except, the Blessed Virgin Mary) in his own flesh (brain and body) and in **community** with others (the world) is born "desacralized."

By personal sins, each of us ratifies or approves of Adam's decision to "desacralize." Also, by sinning, each proves himself to be the offspring of Adam and Eve (II Cor.ll:3) and thus under Adam's curse (under original sin).

Also, each one remains "de-sacralized," and even destined for Hell -- unless and until, God "sacralizes" him. Only God can make any fallen human being so sacred as to be able to live forever partaking of the very life of God.

We are so very fallen that many of us cannot perceive spiritual reality. Obviously, in spite of ecclesial and worldly propaganda to the contrary, **your** flesh (your brain and body) and this world are **EVILMENTAL,** not sacramental. We are not only "sin-full," but we also "naturally" tend to be blind. We are not only blind, but we tend to justify our blindness.

God, in diverse places and in diverse times, from Adam on, has spoken. As it were, God has attempted to save individuals from their "otherwise inevitable destiny."

He has spoken His promises, **His** covenants and His New and Eternal Covenant -- the New Testament Covenant. "Externally or historically," God in various covenants (such as the Adamic promise of the Redeemer, the Noaic promise of mercy, the Abramic promise of a Saviour in his progeny and the Mosaic bond (through God's laws) and through his various prophets (especially the classic biblical prophets) promised, and, as it were, **"pre-presented"** the NEW TESTAMENT COVENANT through which man could become "sacrilized" and ONLY through which man could become "sacrilized." No other door than Christ brings one to Heaven (Acts 4:12).

This NEW TESTAMENT, this NEW COVENANT **in** and **of** the Blood of Christ, God and man, Lord and Saviour resides **in** and comes to us **through** Christ's Catholic Church, outside of which there is **no** salvation. **Extra ecclesiam, nulla salus** isn't a modern day heresy, BUT a **defined dogma** of the **real** Catholic Church.

A Continuing Moral Choice

By **valid** Baptism one enters into the covenant people. By each one's individual moral choices, he/she ratifies or rejects this **initial covenanting.** Covenanting isn't a mechanical or historical choice -- it is a **continuing or on-going moral choice** (a choice that is continually subject to ratification or rejection by those who have attained the age of moral accountability -- this is a defined dogma of the real Catholic Church). As a **continuing moral choice,** covenanting can be rejected -- as long as one remains a moral human being (capable of making moral choices).

At each **valid** Mass, each person is present to the **Sacrifice of Calvary** (**not** a sacred meal or an empty ritual) which is the COVENANT in Christ's Blood. Every time one receives Holy Communion, one receives Christ, God and man, Lord and Saviour in the Eucharist ("which" is indeed Christ - the community is **not** the Eucharist).

70

At each **valid** Mass, one is present "at" the one and only Covenant from God which removes "de-sacrilization" and brings about "sacrilization" -- for each one as he properly responds to God. After reaching the age of moral accountability, no one is "automatically" saved (by some type of past historical or hysterical decision).

Each of us is called to participate in an **ongoing consecration** -- by ratifying his\her initial consecration. As it were, **consecration is LIVING sacred (SECRATION) with (CON) Christ.**

Your consecration means that you CONTINUALLY purpose and live so that: through Christ, with Christ and in Christ you become ever more sacred to God the Father in union with the Holy Spirit now and forever and ever.

Consecration is your only "viable option." Either consecrate and live your Consecration to the Immaculate Heart of Mary and thus to the Sacred Heart of Jesus, **or** go to Hell forever and ever.

Consecration is **your** response to God's Covenant in Christ. Consecration is the renewal of your Baptismal promises in all you **are** and in all you **do**. True consecration will bring you to Heaven. The failure to make and live the true consecration will bring you to an eternal Hell. It's your basic and continuing choice.

The New And Eternal Covenant

At each Mass, each validly ordained priest who has the correct intention *"re-presents"* or makes present again the Saving-Mystery of Christ and His Saving-Being (in the Holy Eucharist).

Each **valid** Mass is defined by the Consecration - the NEW AND ETERNAL COVENANT is made present as Christ's SACRIFICE is re-done in an unbloody manner. At each **valid** Mass, the priest is Christ - Christ renewing and "re-presenting" His Sacrifice.

The last great vision of Sister Lucy occurred at Tuy in 1929.

Here was **the Mass**. Through the Mass, God's GRACE AND MERCY are given to those who would become consecrated to Him. They will adore forever "the Lamb that was slain (Rev. 5:12)" Who is the Essence or focal point of Heaven.

At each Mass, the Lamb is slain "again" for us. The Consecration **is** His Covenant. At each Mass, we who respond to Him by Consecration to Mary and thus to Christ or to Christ through Mary are present at Calvary and receive in Holy Communion the Christ "of Heaven."

The Consecration of the Mass makes your consecration possible. "It" is the Source, Sustainer and Summit of your

personal consecration.

Each validly ordained priest (in the U.S.A. **some** ordinations are invalid when they **exclude** by the intention of the bishop the priest being ordained to offer the sacrifice of Calvary in an unbloody manner at Mass) who validly "says Mass" partakes in the **fullness** of the priestly office - to preserve, guard and hand on what the Founder, Jesus desires.

Each true or faithful priest is so much of a priest that he makes not only Christ present BUT also Christ's Sacrifice. In fact, it is only through Christ's Sacrifice that Christ is made present to us and we **can** be made present in a "positive" way to Christ.

In authentic Catholicism, the priest is Christ's Presence and Power among us. That's why **saints** have told us that if they met an angel and a priest, they would greet the priest first.

Fatima's Consecrations

Today, **how** do you respond to Christ, the Consecrator? How do you respond to Christ's covenant?

You respond to Christ's Covenant by renouncing sin, as well as Satan and all those things that lead to sin. Your renouncement is to be REAL AND CONTINUAL -- it isn't a mental, "worked up" or imagined "Protestant once and for all" acceptance of the idea of Jesus as Savior. Consecration is your **"lived decision"** to be one with Christ in each and every **now** and thus forever and ever.

How is one united to Christ or consecrated to Christ AT EACH MOMENT OF HIS LIFE? By being crucified with Christ (Gal.2:20). Unless you die NOW with Christ, you cannot live with Him, now or forever (Rm.8).

We do not now live the Resurrection. The corpus of the Risen Christ on the cross is a Blasphemous Fantasy. It is Satan's Jesus. It is a futile and sinful "religious" escape from Reality.

By what means are we consecrated to God? By Christ Who came to us through Mary - through Her free will decision to be totally obedient to God the Father. Therefore, we come to Christ through Mary. Mary, in God's Providence, is the one who brought us Christ and who continually brings Christ to us.

Today, we are in the Second Advent - the Advent before Christ's Second Coming. Today, God has spoken through Our Lady of Lourdes and Our Lady of Fatima. The **only** human person who never was "de-sacrilized" is, as it were, the Sign in the Sky preparing us for Him who will come in the sky (Apoc.12).

Mary is the one through whom Christ **came** to us. Mary is the one through whom Christ **now comes** to us. Mary is the one through whom Christ **will come** to us - in the final moment of these end-times or at the hour of our death in these end-times.

Christ loves us through Mary - such is His "freely decided will" or decision. Such a decision is similar to His decisions to come to us through the **waters** poured at a **valid** Baptism and through the bread and wine used at a **valid** Mass. **Certainly** - contrary to the heretical Protestant mindset - Christ can do as **He** desires!

Therefore, in a special way during these end-times of "internal and external" apostasy, it is urgent that you consecrate yourself to Mary - to the Immaculate Heart of Mary - and thus to Jesus: to the Sacred Heart. Such is God's freely determined will.

How do **you** respond to God's will? Do you join Mary and respond in love, gratitude and joy (Lk.1:38)? Or, do you JOIN THE MAJORITY and follow Satan's path of questioning and doubting in order to deny or ignore (Gal.3:1)?

Chapter Nine

True Love Is Consecration

"Love" in Old Testament Hebrew and in New Testament Greek isn't emotional. It's not defined as a feeling - as it is in degenerate societies and religions (especially "American Catholicism"). Feeling-love is sinful love. In fact, it will damn you to an eternal hell (if it is lived for or from).

True love -- as disclosed in GOD'S WORD, the Bible -- is dedication to God through obedience to GOD's will. True love is defined by the Schema Prayer (Dt.6:5) -- love God with all of your being fanatically -- be consecrated to God. Then and only then relate to yourself, your neighbour and all else in the light of or "out of" your total subjection and total obedience (consecration) to God.

In obeying God -- in loving God exclusively and totally -- you truly "love" yourself or see yourself as "relational" -- related to and defined by your total dedication, total obedience and total subjection TO GOD (consecration to God). Being "relational in such a way," you achieve your true dignity - you see yourself as one destined to be -- by God's grace and your graced cooperation -- eternally and infinitely worthwhile. As one who is truly consecrated to God, you are destined to "live in God's life" in infinite and eternal joy, fulfillment, satisfaction, etc.

Your only dignity and your infinite worth come from your total consecration to God. Your infinite and eternal dignity depend on your making and living your consecration to Jesus through Mary or your consecration to Mary and thus to Jesus.

Be consecrated to God. Here, and here alone, is your dignity and worth - infinite and eternal.

Yet, how do you become consecrated? By your will and your strength? Never! Without Christ you can do absolutely nothing.

Covenant-Consecration

Consecration can only come about from God's initiative. Consecration can only be sustained by God's graces. Consecration can only be fulfilled by God's power.

Covenant is God's free gift to save you from eternal damnation. Consecration is your graced response accepting, by word and deed, God's Covenant.

Your consecration comes from, is sustained by and is fulfilled in: THE NEW AND ETERNAL COVENANT IN CHRIST'S BLOOD. At the very Center, Source and Summit of Eternal Life is (both now and forever and ever): "THE LAMB THAT WAS SLAIN (Rev. 5:12; 7:10-12)."

Not only is Christ, Heaven -- Christ is also your **only** way to Heaven (Jn. 6:65, 14:6; 15:4). Being faithful to Christ by Christ's graces and power -- **making and living your awesome personal Fatima Consecration** -- brings you to Heaven (Rv. 12:11).

Covenant-Consecration Through Mary

Christ comes through Mary - the Divinely Feminine Human Person. Such is God's freely chosen plan for the salvation of Eve's children.

You, therefore, should go to Christ through Mary. (In the first advent, Mary brought us Jesus. In the second and definitive advent, Mary again brings Jesus to us and brings us to Jesus.)

Therefore, consecrate yourself to Jesus through Mary, **or** to Mary and **thus** to Jesus. As Immaculate, Mary is "**totally transparent** " to Jesus - all that goes to Her, goes to Jesus and **all** that comes from Jesus to Her for us, goes from Her to us (in as much as each of us can receive God's graces).

Consecrate yourself to the Immaculate Heart of Mary. THUS, according to **God's** will, you will be consecrated to Jesus.

"**Jesus wants to establish in the world devotion to My Immaculate Heart. If you do what I tell you, many souls will be saved**" - Our Lady of Fatima (July 13, 1917).

Is Christ leading **you** to respond to His covenant? Respond by consecration. Respond by a whole-hearted dedication to the Immaculate Heart of Mary. Mary will be your Mother and "Queen" -- to bring you to Jesus and to bring Jesus to you.

Chapter Ten

Consecration To The Immaculate Heart Of Mary: A Contemplation

Mary is defined as THE IMMACULATE CONCEPTION (at the prophecy that prepared us for Fatima - Lourdes, 1858). She **alone**, among human persons **is** Immaculate.

As THE IMMACULATE ONE, She **alone** is **totally obedient** to God (totally and perfectly divinely feminine). As **THE IM-MACULATE HUMAN PERSON**, She, through Her virginity and motherhood, gives us Jesus, and is, as it were, **our Mediatrix with the Mediator.**

You and I can only become Mary's own and **thus** Christ's own in as much as we are like unto Her -- IMMACULATE or sinless -- **or** in as much as we sincerely resolve, by God's grace, to be like Her in Her sinlessness. This is the ultimate goal of our consecrating ourselves to the Immaculate Heart of MARY. **At least** we should resolve to be or to become -- by God's grace and our "graced cooperation" -- free from **mortal sin.**

Do **you** want to consecrate (to become holy with or by Christ's graces as given through Mary) yourself to the Immaculate Heart of Mary? Tell Her -- if you so desire.

The Mother Sanctified By Her Son

The Blessed Virgin Mary is the **only** perfect and **totally** accept-able to God human person. She is such through Her Son Who is Her Lord and Savior in a perfect and total way. Jesus, Lord and Savior, loved His Mother perfectly and totally.

She alone was given the total and perfect salvation - so perfect that She **never** was without its absolute fullness. So total that She **alone** among human persons is the perfect person and therefore the Immaculate Conception.

Christ gave Her the gift of salvation and complete sanctification so fully that there never was **a moment** when She didn't have it -so perfectly did He love His Mother. Therefore, She **is** THE IM-MACULATE CONCEPTION.

Queen Of Martyrs

To help you come to Her and appreciate Her more, realize you are called to be a "co-redeemer" with Christ -- read Col. 1:24. You are called to fill up what is lacking in behalf of others by Christ's sufferings in your body. This mystery is so bold as to be almost unbelievable. Yet, such is the love of the Sacred Heart for us **sinners.**

Imagine His love for the one and only **sinless human person!** As we are blessed to partake in redemption, She is **infinitely more blessed.** Therefore, She is the mediatrix of all graces.

She is also the Queen of Martyrs. The sword of Christ's salvific sufferings pierced Her very Heart. Therefore, we are devoted to Her Immaculate Heart.

The Five Wounds of Christ are Her five wounds - in "imitation, compassion and application." Through Her, they become ours to imitate, to appreciate and to "have applied to us."

Christ Through Mary

At Fatima, as Mary turned Her hands downward, Her children received from Her the grace to see Reality - that sin is the only and ultimate temporal or present evil since sin results in the only ultimate evil of an eternal Hell and that salvation comes through Christ as given to us by His Mother, Mary.

Together with the little children of Fatima, we are called --- by God's grace and our graced cooperation -- to appreciate the Five Wounds. We are also called to have the graces won by Christ's sufferings applied to us.

Lastly, in union with the little children of Fatima, we are called to **"imitate"** the five wounds in order to save ourselves and others from Hell and to be taken to Heaven partaking in God's glory while being forever the greater glory of God.

How do we **"imitate"** the Five Wounds? How did the little children of Fatima **"imitate"** the Five Wounds? Through Mary, we are called to have **hearts** totally dedicated to desiring **only** God and God's will. (We are called to obey the first and greatest commandment.)

Through Mary, we are called to have **hands** that will **do** as God desires. Through Mary, we are called to have **feet** that will **go** where God desires. Lastly, we are called to have placed on our **heads** - and thus "in our minds" -- that Crown of Thorns which will drive out natural evil thoughts and lead us to be transformed by the renewing of our minds in Christ Jesus (Rm. 12:2).

To "imitate" the Five Wounds through Mary, we need to obtain the graces of the Five Wounds through Mary. Of ourselves, we can do **nothing** - nothing worthwhile without Christ's graces given to us through Mary.

Therefore, **be humble!** Pray. Bow your head in humility. Let your heart be "melted down" in subjection. Pray and be devoted to the Immaculate Heart of Mary. Consecrate yourself to Her and **thus** to Jesus. THEN, LIVE YOUR CONSECRATION BY HIS GRACES GIVEN THROUGH HIS CHOSEN VESSEL -- MARY.

Chapter Eleven

Your Urgent Need
To Be Consecrated

Part four of this book will present you with considerations of and meditations on the personal act of consecration to the Immaculate Heart of Mary. Also, three consecration prayers will be given.

You can prepare now for part four by coming to a greater realization of the pressing need that you have to be consecrated to Mary. We are in perilous times. Worst of all, most of us are blind to the perils that surround us or have overcome us.

We not only sin in deed, we sin in habit. We not only sin in habit, we are blind to our sins. Furthermore, most Americans live within the Catholic Church as heretics or apostates (according to a substantial number of reliable surveys).

These **facts** should lead you to flee to the Blessed Virgin for protection. She came in 1917. She came to save us from Hell. How? By consecration to Her Immaculate Heart.

Times will only worsen -- until the proper ecclesial Fatima consecration is done. God has appointed a special providence for our times. **"The holy Rosary and devotion to the Immaculate Heart of Mary are our two last recourses...there will be no others..With a certain trepidation, God offers us the final means of salvation, HIS MOST HOLY MOTHER** (Sister Lucy, the Seer of Fatima)."

Sister Lucy also observes that many bishops and priests are victims of a "diabolic disorientation" which makes them "blind leaders of the blind." Therefore, you will need God's special help not to fall. We close this chapter by considering the remarks of a stigmatist and prophet, Blessed Anna Emmerich, and of a Pope, Pius XII. Meditate on them. Let them lead you to making and living the **awesome Fatima Consecration.**

Anna Catherine Emmerich

Anna Emmerich, nun, mystic and stigmatist, prophesied in 1820. She prophesied that many clerics would be heretics -- deniers of one or more essential teachings of God or of His Church or of any official teaching associated with an "anathema."

"I see **many** excommunicated ecclesiastics who do not seem to be concerned about it or even aware of it. Yet, they are excommunicated...It can be seen thereby that God ratifies the orders, decrees and interdicts issued by the Pope...I saw that those things which pertained to Protestantism gradually gained the upper hand...**Most priests** contributed to the destruction of the Church."

Pope Pius XII

On June 29, 1943, Pope Pius XII confirmed Emmerich's theological position (that one could be excommunicated without being bothered about it or while being blind to one's condition) in his encyclical, MYSTICI CORPORIS.

"Not every sin, even though it be serious, is such as to sever one **automatically** from the body of the church as does schism, heresy or apostasy (p.203)."

Yes, heresy automatically severs one from the Church. Worst of all, many are blind not only to heresy but also to sin. Three Popes --Pius XII, Paul VI and John Paul II -- identify our generation as the one that has lost its sense of sin.

If you have a proper and sane sense of sin and if you believe in the core and essential teachings of the Catholic Church, you are in the minority. You are blessed by God. You are consecrated to Mary.

Therefore, acknowledge this consecration. Become "ever more consecrated." Also, realize that it is only by the special protection of the Blessed Virgin that you will be preserved from destruction in these end-times (Apoc. 12: 13-17) and as Sister Lucy said, "Our Lady will protect all Her dear ones".

PART THREE

THE ECCLESIAL FATIMA CONSECRATION: A CALL TO ACTION

Introduction to Part Three

It might prove helpful for you to "re-read" **THE SPECIAL FOREWORD FOR PART ONE** as it applies to this part of the book as well. Also, once again, you should read chapter three (THE ECCLESIAL FATIMA CONSECRATION - THIS GOD-GIVEN PROPHETIC CHALLENGE IS RESPONDED TO BY SINFUL COVER-UPS).

In this part of the book we reflect on the ecclesial Fatima consecration and its being a call to action-- the hierarchy's and your call to action. At Fatima, in 1917, Our Lady said that She would "come to ask for **the consecration of Russia** to My Immaculate Heart and the Communion of Reparation on the Five First Saturdays. If My requests are heeded, Russia will be converted and there will be peace."

In 1929, Our Lady gave us God's command: "the moment has come when God asks the Holy Father in union with the world's bishops to make **the consecration of Russia to My Immaculate Heart.**" Until this is done, we can expect: "propagation of **Russia's errors** throughout the world, wars, persecutions against Holy Church, the martyrdom of many Christians, various persecutions and sufferings reserved to the Pope, and the annihilation of **several** nations."

Since 1929, reigning pontiffs have done "everything short of obeying God." On March 25, 1984, Pope John Paul II consecrated the world not mentioning Russia and even praying that those people WHO STILL AWAIT OUR CONSECRATION may be enlightened. Since then, until the FALL coverup of 1989, Sister Lucy joined the Pope in admitting the OBVIOUS.

On at least five occasions, before the FALL of 1989, Lucy was asked "Has Russia been consecrated as God demanded at Fatima?" Her clear, "uncomplicated," clearly understandable and explicit answer was: "NO!...NO!...NO!....NO!...NO!" -- always NO!

The Blessed Virgin promised us that "the Holy Father will consecrate **Russia** (properly) to Me and some time of peace will be given to the world."

However, in Sister Lucy's revelation of August 1931, Our Lord complained saying: "They did not wish to heed My demand, like the king of France, **they will repent** and do it, but it will be **late.** Russia will have spread its errors throughout the world, provoking wars and persecutions of the Church. The Holy Father will have much to suffer."

NOW is the time to comply with **God's demands** for the ecclesial Fatima Consecration. **It is now late and as each moment passes, it becomes "even later," yet IT IS NEVER TOO LATE.**

This part of the book consists in a series of reflections or meditations which should motivate you to take proper and effective action in order to bring about **THE AWESOME FATIMA EC- CLESIAL CONSECRATION.** You will notice some "overlap- ping" within these chapters -- try not to let that distract you from their contents.

As consecrated to Mary, work and pray that the proper awesome ecclesial Fatima consecration be done by the Pope and HIS bishops. Work and pray with the absolute assurance of final victory.

Chapter Twelve

The Mega Problem
The Mega Challenge
The Mega Gift; The Mega Solution

Primarily, continually and ultimately **the mega problems** aren't consecration and reparation (and their sacramental Fatima expressions). **Primarily, the mega problem or mega challenge** is whether or not by God's grace you, I and others **CAN REALIZE THAT THE FATIMA MESSAGE IS PROPHETIC -- THAT IT IS FROM GOD AND THAT, AS SUCH, IT MUST BE BELIEVED AND OBEYED.**

Yet, here is **the** mystery - no one **can believe** of himself. Faith is the freely given **gift** of God - lest any man should boast. Belief in the spiritual message and challenge of Fatima is a **mega gift** from God.

Since the Fatima Message and Challenge concern the **basic essentials of life**, our responses to them (personally and ecclesially) become the **mega solutions of life -- temporal and eternal, physical and spiritual; and, personal, as well as communal (or social).**

Our Spiritual Pollution

"Secondarily," the mega problem that we face is the world we live in -- which tends to grossly corrupt our flesh (our brains and bodies). Today, more than in any other period in the history of mankind (I believe and am convinced), you and I are living in the very worst of spiritual situations -- within our (western) church and within our (modern/neo-modern) world. Can **you** see Reality? Do **you** see what I see (by God's gift of faith)?

Do YOU perceive this basic message of Fatima? Mankind -- modern mankind -- is SPIRITUALLY ROTTEN. "Many living today will be in Hell forever and ever" -- The Fatima Message. **The Hearts of Jesus and Mary are greatly grieved and offended about OUR BEHAVIOR.**

This is a basic part of the awesome message of Fatima. God's contemporary challenge DEMANDS your response? Will it be positive? Will it be negative?

Will you do what YOU can to solve -- by God's gifts of His

graces -- the primary and secondary mega problems? For your own personal good, will you embrace God's Fatima-given mega solution? "For" Jesus and Mary and for the true good of others and of yourself -- will you embrace God's Fatima-given mega solution?

Will you positively respond by embracing the awesome personal Fatima Consecrations (and their implied and required reparations)? Will you positively respond by supporting and promoting the proper awesome ecclesial Fatima Consecration of Russia? You can only respond positively by God's gift of faith.

For those without God's gift of faith and/or acceptance and living such a gift-- the Real Fatima Message, at least, comes as something unimportant or unproved; and, "at most," comes to them as the enemy that must be opposed and defeated, even by lies and cover-ups.

If you are living in the modern and liberal apostate-controlled American, Canadian, French etc. "Catholic" church, you live in horrible "spiritual excrement." Are you graced to see this? If you are living in such a spiritual situation, you are undergoing a GREAT TEST (crisis) which with the proper grace-given and free responses will make you into a great saint, now and forever.

Faith makes visible the unseen spiritual world (Hb 11:3). Once it is made visible, you can be victorious if you live by faith - faith is also your victory (1 Jn. 5:4).

The Fatima Message is the Fatima Challenge. Its consecration/reparation content is gratefully and eagerly embraced by "God's elect"-- those who live by faith (Hb. 10:38).

Also, each of God's elect have or "are given" the EVANGELIZING HEARTS of Jesus and Mary. They will spread the Fatima Message. They will consecrate themselves as well as pray and work for the consecration of others-- especially of RUSSIA AS GOD COMMANDED AT FATIMA.

A Pope-Saint Predicts:

In closing this chapter, it will be edifying for us to cite the words of Pope St. Pius X. He spoke "prophetically" in his inaugural encyclical, "E Supremi Apostolatus Cathedra", Oct. 4, 1903. Notice how he acknowledges and predicts the internal apostasy which we are experiencing in its fullness in our day.

Notice also how he realizes and confirms that the Pope is set over nations and kingdoms to tear down or to build up. Indeed, the Pope -- not the Head of Russia or the man-appointed world leader -- is **THE VICAR OF CHRIST AND THE VICAR OF MANKIND.**

This pontifical address of 1903 was a prelude to Fatima (1917). The Pope is the Vicar of Christ **and** the Vicar of mankind. As he **obeys** God's Fatima **DEMAND, OR COMMAND,** regarding RUSSIA, Russia and the world will **truly** prosper. As he continues to **disobey** God's **COMMAND** as given at Fatima, Russia and the world will worsen -- physically and spiritually, temporally and eternally; and, individually as well as communally (or socially).

"We felt a sort of terror, considering the disastrous conditions of humanity at the present hour. Can we ignore such a profound and grave evil, which at this moment much more than in the past, is working away at its very marrow and leading it to its ruin? You know what this malady is, Venerable Brethren, it is **the abandoning of God and apostasy from Him;**... We understood that **it belongs to Us, in virtue of the pontifical office entrusted to Us, to provide a remedy for such a great evil. We believe that this order of God was addressed to Us: 'Behold, today I set you over nations and kingdoms, to tear down and destroy, to build up and to plant...(Jer. 1: 10).'**

...Truly, whoever ponders these things must necessarily and firmly fear whether such a perversion of minds is not **the sign announcing the beginning of the last times,** and that the Son of Perdition spoken of by the Apostle (II Thess.2,3) might already be living on this earth.... religion is mocked everywhere, and the dogmas of the faith are fought against, there is a stubborn effort to completely suppress man's duties towards God! Now this, according to the same Apostle, is the character proper to Antichrist. **Man, with unspeakable temerity, has usurped the place of the Creator,** lifting himself above everything that bears the name of God. It has reached such a point that, being powerless to completely extinguish in himself the notion of God, he nevertheless shakes off the yoke of His Majesty, and dedicates the visible world to himself in the guise of the temple, where he pretends to receive the adoration of his own kind...'**He sits in the temple of God, and gives himself out as if he were God (II Thess.2,4).'"** [**E Supremi Apostolatus Cathedra, Pope Saint Pius X, Oct. 4, 1903**]

89

Chapter Thirteen

Consecrating Yourself; Consecrating Russia

Consecrating yourself/consecrating Russia, emphasizes God's view of reality and your subsequent role or responsibility. How is this true?

From God's view of reality, ALL is God's and ALL is determined by God. Therefore, by grace are you saved and not by your ability and efforts.

YET, you are saved freely (a mysterious sort of hypothetical necessity exists) - you must choose to be saved by your desires and deeds to obey God or not. Such freedom constitutes YOUR INFINITE RESPONSIBILITY AND YOUR INFINITE DIGNITY, You determine by your obedience or failure to obey your eternal existence in Heaven or Hell.

Consecrating yourself/consecrating Russia, also emphasizes your role or your responsibility. Your choice in life is to break out of being under Adam's curse and to come under Christ's blessing, OR "naturally" to live in a cursed world and cursed flesh and go to Hell.

Consecrate yourself to Mary. Live the Fatima Message. Sister Lucy assures us that God will lead the Church to consecrate Russia as He desires "when a sufficient number of people are complying with the Message of Fatima."

Your basic choice in life is to live the Fatima Message or live "naturally" and go to Hell. Choose Mary as your Mother or ratify Eve as your mother.

Today, in these Marian days, your choice is to naturally ratify or to "grace-fully" break with the "Eve-spirit." EVE is naturally the mother of all (Gn. 3:20). As such, she is naturally your mother. SHE ,as it were, AS YOUR EARTH MOTHER (THE MOTHER OF YOUR FLESH AND THE WORLD) will bring you to eternal misery in Hell.

HOW do you break with the "Eve-spirit?" By God's grace and your "grace-filled" (or graced) cooperation, you can consecrate yourself to MARY. [Consecration is freely and "gracefully" choosing the "Mary-spirit" and rejecting the "Eve-spirit."]

As it were, by nature, Eve is your mother (the "giver" and nurturer of life); and, Mary, by your "God-graced" choice, will be your Mother. **This** is the Fatima Challenge AND Blessing -- both personal and ecclesial -- to "make" Mary our Mother.

MARY is that human person who alone is: The Divinely Feminine One (in contrast to Eve who epitomizes the diabolically feminine one), the Immaculate One, the Virgin, the Mother of God and your Mother (by devotion and consecration) who comes to us today as the Sign in the Heavens (see my Marian Meditations for a more complete description of devotion to Mary) -- Our Lady of Fatima.

These are called "Marian Days" by Pope John Paul II. They are the end-times. **These** are the times of the second and definitive Advent. For the second coming of Christ, Mary has been given a prominent role. "In **these end-times**, God wishes to establish in a special way, devotion to the Immaculate Heart of Mary" -- Fatima.

What does consecrating **yourself** have to do with consecrating Russia? As we already pointed out, God will grant the consecration of Russia when a sufficient number of **INDIVIDUALS** are living the Fatima message - the awesome personal consecration.

The Pope We Deserve?

God's view of history (which is the **only** view of any real importance) places **one** man or woman as responsible for the fate of many (e.g. Mary, Adam, Eve, Abraham, Moses, David, etc). **Today** (A.D. -- in the year of **Our Lord**), this **one** man on earth is the Pope. He represents us to God even as he represents God to us.

He is **our** Vicar **and** Christ's Vicar on earth. Yet, in general, we tend to get as Pope the "Pope we deserve" for better or for worse.

As the Pope decides, so go the "externals" of the spiritual and temporal dimension of Catholicism and of the whole world. Such is the Pope's dignity and responsibility. Our Lady of Fatima confirms this as She relays to him God's command that he order the consecration of Russia (to be done as God desires).

As you read this, the Pope is probably continuing in his disobedience towards God (i.e. towards God's will as given to us at Fatima). Why, then, consecrate **yourself** to Mary?

The Blessed Virgin in recent times has manifested Herself to us as REALISTIC LOVE (or "tough love"). She lovingly or "caringly" tells each and every individual that he/she is "**sinfully rotten**" and deserves God's **special** punishments **unless** he leads a life of prayer, obedience, mortifications and conversion (coming to faith and growing in faith). or, in effect, **unless he consecrates himself to the Immaculate Heart of Mary.**

Winning The War -- Not Just A Few Battles

By God's grace, I have been led to join authentic Catholics in defending and protecting the Catholic Faith against its internal enemies -- bishops, priests, theologians and experts. In doing this, I have experienced a sense of: "What's the use?"

We, the militantly orthodox, **at best,** win very few battles. We are losing the war!

For the war to be won requires special intervention by the Holy Spirit which is obtained through our Fatima consecrations. Here, alone, is our hope of final and complete victory.

As we live our consecrations, we will be as we should be. All that we say and do will be all that we could say and do.

Then, as a sufficient number of us live our consecrations (by what we say and do), God has assured us that He will "overwhelmingly grace" a Pope to obey His ecclesial Fatima Command. Yet, what happens if the Pope continues to disobey God's Fatima Command?

Winners Can't Lose

As you obey God personally (especially by God's chosen end-times devotion of consecration to Mary), you will win either way. If the Pope continues to disobey God regarding the ecclesial consecration of Russia, Mary will fortify you to become a saint in "the worst of times." On the other hand, if the Pope FINALLY comes to obey God, and consecrates Russia as God desires, Mary will fortify you to become a saint "in the best of times."

All works together for YOUR good -- provided you make and live the AWESOME PERSONAL CONSECRATION. All works together for mankind; and, especially, Russia -- when a sufficient number of individuals have made and are living their awesome personal consecrations.

Then, we are promised by God, God's "super-sufficient" and totally effective graces will be given to the Pope and HIS bishops to finally do GOD'S WILL: TO MAKE THE AWESOME ECCLESIAL FATIMA CONSECRATION OF RUSSIA TO THE IMMACULATE HEART OF MARY.

Therefore, consecrate yourself to Our Lady. Live this consecration.

93

Live in the pure light of Fatima. Live the Fatima Message. Live in hope -- realizing that one great day, the Pope will obey God and consecrate **RUSSIA** as God desires. **Live the Fatima Challenge -- do all you can do to bring about obedience to GOD'S DEMANDS as given to us at Fatima: to make the awesome personal and ecclesial Fatima consecrations.**

Victory Is Assured

When the Pope makes the awesome ecclesial Fatima Consecration -- you will live within a church which once again is faithful and "faith-filled" in bringing Christ to each person and each person to Christ.

Rejoice in the promises of Fatima. One day, one wonderful day in the future (we hope and pray that it will be in the not too distant future), God assures us that a Pope will finally obey God and make the AWESOME ECCLESIAL FATIMA CONSECRATION OF RUSSIA TO THE IMMACULATE HEART OF MARY.

Our prayers will then be answered. Our efforts will then "be paid off." Hope will be realized! YOU AND ALL INDIVIDUALS OF THIS PLANET will be blessed. Russia will be blessed. INDIVIDUALS throughout the world will be blessed.

On that wonderful day in the future all mankind will realize and see that the Catholic Church is the one and only means of salvation. Extra ecclesiam, nulla salus - will no longer be considered to be a "post Vatican Two" heresy, but will be reaffirmed as an essential and perennial dogma of the one true Church of Christ: the Catholic Church.

When Russia is finally consecrated as God demands, everyone will perceive that not only does **salvation** come through the Catholic Church (the Pope, especially); but also, well-being, peace and safety for Catholics as well as for the whole world. **This is the awesome Message, Challenge and Blessing of Fatima.**

Therefore, now (as the Fatima Consecration is **not** done), live, pray and work that it may be done.

Sister Lucy once wrote: "I asked Our Lord why He would not convert Russia without the Holy Father making the specified Consecration. He replied **'Because I want My whole Church to acknowledge that** *consecration* **as a triumph of the Immaculate Heart of Mary, so that it may extend Her cult later on and put devotion to the Immaculate Heart beside devotion to My Sacred**

Heart.' "

Also, Our Lord said: "Pray much for the Holy Father...given they [the Pope and bishops] follow the example of the King of France in delaying the execution of My command, they will follow him into misfortune."

In 1931, Our Lord assured Sr. Lucy that the Pope would "repent" and make the proper Fatima ecclesial consecration "but it will be late."

"In the end, My Immaculate Heart will triumph the Holy Father will Consecrate Russia to Me. Russia will be converted and a period of peace will be given the world" - Our Lady of Fatima. **CONSECRATING YOURSELF/CONSECRATING RUSSIA WILL BRING TRUE PEACE TO ALL OF THE INDIVIDUALS OF THIS WORLD.**

Chapter Fourteen

A Meditation On The Ecclesial Fatima Consecration As The Radical Choice

At the base or foundation of the present "MAN-affirming" and subsequent "MAN by MAN-governed" religio-political mindset is the affirmation of MAN as God and the denial of GOD as GOD -- GOD of man and all other creatures.

However, in affirming MAN and denying GOD, **man** is trivialized and trashed. As St. Iraeneus once stated: "only a man who is fully alive to God glorifies GOD and **thus** himself."

Conversely, in denying God or in failing to acknowledge God as God, one trivializes and trashes himself. In exalting Man as God, the sought-after God-like glory soon sours into HATE which breeds **irresponsibility** towards oneself and all others as well as a trivializing and trashing of one's own **dignity** and the dignity of others.

True responsibility is denied by every "broadly defined" Communist or every "communist" as spelled with a small "c" [which we use to include: socialists, "Catholic" socialists, secular humanists and New Agers]. This small "c" communism is what Our Lady refers to as "RUSSIA'S ERRORS."

All of these small "c" communists (from bishops to laypeople) deny the RESPONSIBILITY and thus the DIGNITY of each human being. Therefore, the REAL CATHOLIC CHURCH solemnly and dogmatically teaches that no one can be a communist and a true follower of Christ.

Our Lady of Fatima has challenged and continues to challenge Popes and bishops to consecrate **Russia** - to admit communism is wrong and needs to be exorcised from "Red Russia" and from the rest of the world. Thus, the Pope -- along with **HIS** bishops -- will affirm GOD "over MAN" which will result in lovingly bending their knees to GOD (not MAN); living from and for LOVE (not hate); and, most of all, affirming the "awful" God-given and God-directed (**not** Man-given and Man-directed) RESPONSIBILITY and DIGNITY of each person.

The "Awesomeness" Of
The Radical Choice

Indeed, Fatima presents us with **the radical choice** (which Pope Saint Pius X so clearly foresaw -- as we have seen). The Pope, representing us, will finally make the radical choice -- **to affirm God as God and to renounce MAN as GOD.**

As a concrete result of such an action, the mega-force which affirms MAN as GOD will be destroyed. "Red Russia" will once more become Holy Russia. Also, Rome will once again be restored to its prior glory. No longer will Rome be held captive by MAN and **thus** by Satan.

Can't you begin to see why some bishops and other "church leaders" (mostly, in the "West") don't really want to consecrate Russia to the Immaculate Heart of Mary as God commanded? They'd have to denounce and repudiate their own man-originating, man-pleasing, man-directed and "man-goaled" DIRECTIONS as expressed in their "dogmatically decreed" and "dictatorially imposed" theories, policies, procedures, practices and programs.

For these "rotten church leaders," IT'S TOO BIG A PRICE TO PAY. These evil leaders refuse to affirm GOD AS GOD and to affirm man as sinful and subservient to God. They are adamant in affirming MAN as God and/or MAN with God subservient to him.

Can't you see why a sizeable number of bishops (yet, a minority) in their right God-affirming minds and hearts **actively and positively** desire to consecrate Russia **as** God **obliges them to do.** For **them** -- for these faith-filled and faithful (to God and **not** to man) zealous bishops -- God is God and **Man** isn't God.

Such an affirmation is a **basic** part of **their** prayer life - their relating to God in the depths of their souls. **They** rejoice in praying as God **commands** them to pray by consecrating Russia in the proper way. **They** thank God for the great Fatima opportunity. They work hard to bring about the **awesome ecclesial Fatima consecration.**

For now, it would seem, we have a "controlling number" of **evil** bishops and/or Pope. **These** are faithless and/or unfaithful (to God and to His Blessed Mother).

As Our Lady sees this, She weeps. She is sad. Her statues weep. In the Ukraine, She appeared in **black.** At Fatima, She appeared saddened by sins. Today, Our Lady is **not** smiling.

According to Malachi Martin (in THE KEYS OF THIS BLOOD), Our Lady requested that the Pope of 1960 (Pope John XXIII) disclose the Third Secret - which insisted on the ecclesial Fatima consecration being made as God demanded. Pope John XXIII chose not to obey God.

Why? Largely out of fear of offending MAN in the form of Red Russia. After all, the proper awesome ecclesial Fatima consecration makes RUSSIA the object of a "special exorcism" or consecration. The Communists would be insulted and even consider such a consecration as an act of war.

Call To Action

Therefore, we suffer (until the Pope obeys God). We suffer: wars, famines, persecutions and the annihilation of nations. The world suffers from the spread of RUSSIA'S ERRORS -- the spread of small "c" communism (socialism, secular humanism, "Catholic" socialist thinking and the "New Age" movement). The Church suffers persecutions (internal, especially), demonic delusions and internal apostasy. The Pope suffers -- internally, and perhaps even "externally" (as predicted by God). Worst of all, souls go to Hell -- since a sufficient number of us don't make and live the AWESOME FATIMA CONSECRATION in order that the Pope may be "graced into" obeying God's Fatima Command.

As time goes on - until the Pope finally comes to obey God - we suffer more and more. A demonic spirit deludes and destroys us. A demonic (MAN-AFFIRMING) spirit even seems to control certain parts of the Vatican.

Worse yet, as time goes on, the prognosis seems to become ever more dismal. As our world decays morally so do our bishops (indeed, 1960 was the best time - in the past - as Our Lady indicated).

However, NOW is our only time of "grace." Therefore NOW is the best present time to make and live your Fatima Consecration so that a sufficient number of dedicated souls can exist which will assure that the Pope will be "graced into" obeying God's Fatima Command. Also, "push" for the consecration of RUSSIA. "Force" your bishop, at least, to act as if he believes in Jesus and Mary and is faithful to them.

At least, in your name and in the name of the "faithfilled" and faithful of his diocese, he should actively work to bring about the proper ecclesial consecration of Russia to the Immaculate Heart of

Mary as **GOD** has commanded at Fatima. To begin with, he should express his dedication to GOD'S FATIMA-GIVEN WILL both publicly and to the Pope.

Push your bishop to be **your** representative (and the representative of like-minded and "like-hearted" true Catholics). Keep pushing until he **does** what is right and just.

Also, NOW is the time to push the Pope, into consecrating **Russia** to the Immaculate Heart of Mary as God demanded over **sixty** years ago. The longer the delay, the more horrible the just (and merciful) punishments from God (according to Our Lady of Fatima).

Even on the "natural plane," you can envisage the results of such a consecration. Evil empires, ultimately, are built on **the fundamental lie that MAN without God determines his own destiny.** They live in fear of the truth. They hate the truth. They constantly suppress the exposure of the truth.

A TOTALLY LETHAL EXPOSURE TO TRUTH would occur in the very act of properly consecrating Russia. [No wonder (according to Malachi Martin) Pope John the Twenty-third perceived the Fatima ecclesial consecration as a "declaration of war" on Russia.]

Every communistic government (including the socialistic nations of U.S.A. and Canada) enslaves its subjects. Slavery demeans the enslaved as it reduces them to being responsible to Man (the ruling clique) and not to God and looking to Man (the ruling clique) to define each one's dignity or worth towards the community - which in turn is defined by the ruling clique. Indeed, such communistic slavery is the worst of slaveries as it entices and leads individuals to consider themselves as "animals belonging to the state" instead of as endowed by their Creator with inalienable dignity, responsibility and rights.

Likewise, **every** communistic government (and **increasingly** the U.S.A.) suppresses God-directed religion - especially that which is THE religion revealed by God for men to follow: the Catholic Church.

In these end-times, Our Lady of Fatima is God's chosen instrument to enact special salvation. She wants to save Her children from the Red Dragon (Rv.:12) which is intent on trivializing and trashing them, both in time and in eternity (now and forever), by taking away God-given responsibility and dignity and substituting a frustrating and therefore hateful and hate-filled man-given responsibility and "dignity" (meditate on this paragraph and on Rev. 12 ; 13).

Have you done what you can do to get the Pope and bishops of God's one and only true Church - the Catholic Church - to repent and to represent you by complying with your God-inspired wishes?

Why not? Certainly the consequences are important since they are infinite. Certainly, the task is simple! How much more simple can it be than to consecrate RUSSIA to the Immaculate Heart of Mary in a spirit of reparation and endorsing reparation? Certainly, the cause is good and proper.

Remember, the (theological) liberals destroyed the true church in your parish and in your diocese by pushing. They weren't satisfied until they got their evil will to be done on earth (according to Satan's plan in Hell). Why should you be satisfied with excuses and "cover-ups?" Push. Push like the liberals pushed.

I challenge you to be even "one-tenth" as dedicated to God as this generation is dedicated to its own diabolic "man" causes (Lk. 16:8). Push, as if all depends on you. Pray, realizing God is supreme. Push and Pray! Don't be satisfied until Our Lady of Fatima's simple yet awesome heavenly command is fulfilled.

On December 26, 1957, Sister Lucia, surviving seer of Fatima, in an interview with Father Fuentes, well known Fatima priest stated: "Father, the Most Holy Virgin is very sad, because nobody is concerned about Her message, the good as well as the evil. Tell them, Father, that the Holy Virgin has told me many times, as also Francisco and Jacinta, that many nations will disappear from the face of the earth. She has said that Russia will be the scourge, chosen by Heaven to chastise the entire world, if we do not obtain beforehand the conversion of that poor nation."

It is now over sixty years since the initial Fatima Message. The world is farther removed than ever from the so ardently hoped-for peace -- peace for souls and "bodies," eternal and temporal, spiritual and material.

Yet, we who are truly consecrated to Mary are blessed to work and pray WITH ASSURANCE OF VICTORY. A ray of hope penetrates the present darkness: "In the end, My Immaculate Heart will triumph. The Holy Father will consecrate Russia to me. It will be converted and a period of peace will be granted to the world" -- Our Lady of Fatima.

Which Holy Father will finally do God's will? Which people of God will be responsible by their prayers and actions - for "pushing" the Pope into doing God's will? Will you be one of Mary's special children? Will you share in Her inevitable victory?

Meditate and pray. Try to realize that the radical choice which the awesome Fatima Challenge presents to us is to deny MAN AS GOD and to reaffirm -- in spirit and in truth as well as totally and exclusively -- that **GOD IS GOD** and all that such an affirmation implies.

Chapter Fifteen
The Representative Model

Let's pause and re-examine what we have already seen. God has freely chosen throughout the history of mankind to have the fate of communities of men be in the hands of **one person**. Such is God's will.

God has freely chosen to have groups of people represented by **one** person. As Adam went, so went the whole human race - through **one** man's sin, death (physical and spiritual) entered the whole human race (except, of course, for the Blessed Virgin Mary).

In dealing with His chosen people, God worked through one man. **Moses,** David and the other Kings - each of these stood for the people of Israel.

As Moses went, so went Israel. **Conversely,** as the people went, so went Moses. Moses and the Kings of Israel, represented the people - for good or for evil.

Today, Fatima assumes and builds on **this** foundation or fundamental "assumption." The Pope represents not only Catholicism - the one true religion and its followers - but, also mankind.

If and when **the Pope** obeys God's command given through Our Lady of Fatima, the Church and mankind will be blessed and preserved from greater physical and spiritual harm. It's up to the Pope as **our REPRESENTATIVE.** His choices gravely affect all of us.

Therefore, each of us has a right and a "pressing urgency" to insist that the presently reigning Pope AS THE REPRESENTATIVE OF MANKIND do what God commands - for our own temporal and eternal well-being and for the temporal and eternal well-being of others.

Ghandi observed that, in general, we get the government we deserve. It is also true that, in general, we get the church leadership we deserve - by our actions or by our failure to act.

Never let anyone (even a Cardinal or a Vatican official) convince you that you have no right to "bother the Pope into doing" what is for your own good. This right is not only inalienable; but, also, it becomes your duty towards God IN TRUE LOVE TOWARDS YOURSELF AND OTHERS -- on behalf of yourself and others. Not only should we do what we can in the "natural order," we should also do what we can in the "spiritual domain."

We pray to Mary asking Her to help our Holy Father to join Her -- in spirit and in truth -- in bringing God's blessings to mankind. May God inspire the Holy Father to imitate Mary by being the slave of God - doing and being done to **as God desires.**

Just as Mary's perfect obedience brought us our greatest blessing -Christ, our Savior - so also, to a far lesser and yet to a tremendously important extent, the Pope's obedience will bring us the great blessings of Fatima and prevent us from suffering the "full curse of Fatima."

Pope - Vicar Of God And Vicar Of Man

"**Pope John-Paul II very soon learned of Our Lady of Fatima's request. In 1980, in the course of a meal and in the presence of Cardinal Wyszynski, Mgr. Hnilica informed him that: 'the most important act he would have to do during his pontificate would be the consecration of Russia to the Immaculate Heart of Mary in union with all the bishops.'**

John-Paul II replied that 'the Russians would regard such a consecration as an interference in their internal affairs...' Furthermore, he objected, 'the Pope's jurisdiction only encompasses the Catholic Church, and that the Pope is not Pope of all men.'

Cardinal Wyszynski replied that 'Christ being the King of the whole world, His vicar had jurisdiction over all men.' Brother Michael has shown that 'the doctrinal justification for the act requested at Tuy in 1929 is already to be found clearly expounded in Leo XIII's encyclical 'Annum Sacrum of 25 May 1899.'

Contrary to what has been affirmed by certain theologians, there is no dogmatic difficulty "in the Pope and the Catholic bishops consecrating schismatic and Bolshevik Russia without any participation on the part of its authorities either ecclesial or political". In this conversation with John-Paul II, Cardinal Wysznski did no more than repeat the teaching of Leo XIII." [The above paragraphs were taken from *Catholic Counter Reformation* No. 227 - p.15].

In a day when the church is self-destructing from A LACK OF PROPER UNITY which originates from the Pope (**most** American "Catholics" do not believe in papal infallibility), God assures us by The Fatima Consecration that the **Pope** is **not** "the first bishop among equals" (**primus inter paribus**) but that he and he alone **is** the Vicar of Christ on earth. What **he** binds on earth is bound in

Heaven and what **he** looses on earth is loosed in Heaven (Mt. 16:19). He and he alone is **the** Pope.

The Pope and only the Pope - by himself - is the Vicar of Christ on earth. The Fatima Consecration is built on **this** truth. As **he** in control of and in union with his bishops (the bishops who refuse to join with **him** could be removed by **him**) speaks and acts, God is bound to act - God will loose His curses and bind His blessings. Such is the Power of Christ's Vicar on earth. The Pope is **unique**-- he fully possesses the power of Christ on earth. **No** one else has such fullness of Power.

Also, the Pope - and **only** the Pope - is **the** Vicar of **all humans.** As he conforms to God's will, humanity is blessed. As he continues in disobedience to God's will that Russia be consecrated to the Immaculate Heart of Mary by the Pope, in union with his bishops - all humans suffer: physically and/or spiritually, temporally and/or eternally. The Head of Russia or the Head of the New Age World is **not** or will not be the Vicar of Men-- such a one is a LIAR and a MURDERER.

The Fatima Consecration affirms and ratifies God's will - that the Pope, and the Pope alone, is the Vicar of Christ on earth and the Vicar of men. What an awesome meaning the consecration has! IT IS NOT ONLY A PROFESSION OF REALITY, BUT ALSO A PROFESSION OF THE CATHOLIC CHURCH AS THE ONE AND ONLY TRUE CHURCH FOUNDED BY JESUS CHRIST AND AS NECESSARY FOR SALVATION.

The Fatima Consecration, by itself, **cures** the central cause of the church's **self-destruction.** Only a Pope like Pope St. Pius X can reinstitute UNITY according to **God's** model of unity. Only a **saintly** Pope will be bold enough to obey God and not MAN.

We now work and pray (with assurance of victory) for the "emergence" of such a Pope. When such a Pope "materializes," then national bodies of bishops, individual bishops and each priest or "legitimate priest representative" once more will be governed by the Pope. No longer will heresy be rewarded and thus flourish. Heresy will be squelched as it was during the reign of the Saint and Pope -- Pope St. Pius X. ANARCHY (apostasy within) will cease and the Catholic Church will once more EXIST AS, be perceived to be and function as: ONE ... **and thus HOLY, UNIVERSAL (Catholic) and APOSTOLIC.**

How? By the Fatima Consecration. Such a consecration will affirm that the Pope and **only** the Pope is the Head of the Church. **TRUE UNITY will supplant the prevailing lawlessness and**

**anarchy. Indeed, the ecclesial Fatima Consecration is
AWESOME.**

Chapter Sixteen
The Divine Paradox Of Fatima's Ecclesial Peace Plan

"Whosoever shall seek to save his life, shall lose it (Lk. 17:33) ... ["Unless the grain of wheat falling into the ground die, itself remaineth alone."] (Jn. 12:24) ... "What doth it profit a man to gain the whole world, and suffer the loss of his own soul?" (Mt. 16:25)

If you love mankind, you will not love Man, even if it seems to run against or go contrary to those who profess Man as their goal/god. But if you love God and do what He commands then you will truly love man. It's that simple. It's that paradoxical. It's that awesome.

Pray for the Pope. "Push" the Pope. Insist that he in union with the bishops of the world on one day consecrate RUSSIA to the Immaculate Heart of Mary. Insist that he does what God commands through Our Lady of Fatima.

These are your rights and duties - to pray and work so that God's will be done on earth to bring about His Heavenly Peace Plan. **Peace** is promised **us** by the **obedience** of the Pope in union with **his** bishops.

What kind of peace? Temporal and/or eternal peace - for yourself and others. Temporal peace for the church and for nations. Otherwise, nations, the church, others and you yourself will suffer -- eternally and/or temporally.

Certainly, peace is worthwhile. All we need to do is pray for the Pope and **work** so that he will embrace the divine paradox and, as it were, be embraced by Mary.

Which Holy Father will **finally** embrace the **divine** paradox? **Which** people of God will be responsible - by their prayers and action - for "pushing" the Pope into embracing the Divine Paradox? Will **you** be one of Mary's special children?

Chapter Seventeen

The Politico-Religious Mega-Sin

There's a story told about a man who discovered one of his wheels wasn't attached to the car. The mechanic had forgotten to put the nuts on. He happened to stop outside of an insane asylum.

Being nervous, he told the man behind the fence about his problem. The crazy man told him to take a nut from each of the other three wheels and put it on the loose one.

The driver was astonished. "I thought you were crazy," he said. "I am, but I'm not stupid," replied the crazy man.

Likewise, Satan and his evil pawns - Russia and its enslaved empires - aren't **stupid**, they're **evil.** In fact, **they** are far more devious and alert than are the Pope, bishops, church leaders and the national leaders of the major powers of the free world. Far, far more devious, alert, intelligent, cunning, diplomatic, crafty, etc.- are evil people (Lk. 16:8).

Satan is even victorious **within** the Catholic Church. Among Satan's greatest enemies are the Mass, the Eucharist and true devotion to Mary. Look what he's done to the Mass by way of the Man-affirming "nearly heretical **Novus Ordo.**"

As a **result** of the **Novus Ordo** and the present mindset, look what's happened to Jesus in His Eucharistic Presence. **Adoration** of the Eucharist is treated as an heretical or outmoded and evil practice by many of the apostate bishops and priests within "Catholicism." Jesus is "kicked out of" His churches -- as tabernacles are emptied and/or moved.

Look what the devil and his followers have done to Mary. A simple **divine** command given through Mary has yet to be done after more than one half of a century. Satan's **not** dumb, he's evil. Satan's not only evil, he's victorious.

The Present Scenario

On the political front, Russia skillfully employs (or, has **recently** skillfully employed) its sixth glasnost as it maintains its offensive arsenal at our expense. We don't want to or **"can't"** comprehend the fact that evil is evil and **not** dumb.

We are dumb before evil's cleverness - we even **support** the evil empire. How dumb can one be? As it were, we are blinded by

Satan - yet, in reality, we are **not** graced by God to see Truth. We are cursed by God (cf. Rm. 1:18-2:4).

On the ecclesial front, the one and only Church of Christ - Who is the one and only Way of Salvation from sin and Hell - seems to be paralysed in fear or "shock" by evil. It can't and/or won't obey God's simple command in order to attain world peace - for itself and for mankind.

Instead, it embraces Satan's "politico-religious" lie - that **MAN** must be the focal point of religion and, therefore, (small "c") communism becomes OUR SAVIOR. God and God's Will no longer hold **the** central focus of religion - not even of Catholicism (at least, in its "Western expression"). No doubt, the church has become **political** - and it has done so in a **sinful** way.

Therefore, the controlling force within the Catholic Church **must** change its present direction. That's **the** essential ecclesial message and challenge of Fatima. Our Lady of Fatima wishes to help lead the Church to see and to repent of its **"mega politico-religious SIN."**

The ruling authorities -the Pope and the Catholic bishops (<u>not</u> the schismatic orthodox bishops) - must change their mindset. They are commanded by God at Fatima to renounce their political role and to reassume their proper religious role. They are commanded to put God and God's will before MAN.

They are commanded to put **God** before Man. They are commanded to **express** this commitment by doing exactly what God commands through Our Lady of Fatima.

Pray for the ruling authorities of Catholicism. They too are enslaved to a pro-Man and **thus** a pro-Satan mindset. Many of them even seem to have been deluded into believing that to be pro-Man is to be pro-God and not pro-Satan.

At Fatima, Mary urged us to **pray** for the Pope. She also said, in effect, that his **sin** -- his ongoing **sin** of disobeying God and failing to honor Mary as **God** desires -- would bring about his own sufferings and persecutions.

Why does the Pope disobey God? He fears MAN and not God (unless he is inculpably ignorant of the Fatima Message). Indeed, St. Thomas Acquinas was correct in his prediction that one of the last temptations for the upper clergy will be to become POLITICAL -- to put MAN before God.

Pray for the Pope. Pray that he may be "spiritually" enlightened to see that he is a prisoner of a mega evil force within the church. Pray that he may have the courage to make, as it were, a blind leap of faith into Mary's waiting arms and do

exactly as God commands through Our Lady of Fatima - consecrate RUSSIA properly.

Pray for your bishop and pray and encourage him to free himself from the mega evil force to denounce the worship of Man by perceiving and rejecting RUSSIA'S ERRORS (especially in the form of small "c" communism and the exaltation of MAN over God) which are corrupting our church and society.

Pray that he may consecrate **your** diocese to Mary. Encourage him to do so. **Insist** -- with the persistence of liberal evil forces -- that he do so.

Do the same regarding **your** pastor and **your** parish (in a sense, the hierarchy is representative - representative of you for your good as God desires, not as evil liberal forces desire). Support -- by prayer, financially, etc. -- those organizations which are presently working to disclose the Fatima Message and to bring about obedience to it (at present, in the U.S.A., less than two percent of Catholics know about Fatima and less than half of them know the Real Fatima Message and the truth about our reactions to it).

Also, make this consecration yourself and for your family. After all, in doing so, you are "merely" renewing the **vows** of your Baptism with the special assistance of the Blessed Virgin Mary. That's the least you can do. That the "least" you MUST DO.

Lastly, as we have seen, the Pope **also** is **your** representative. As such, you have every right (and a present duty before God) to **insist** he **act** on your behalf for your own good, the good of others, for the glory of God and in a special way for God's glory as shown through Mary. In these perilous end-times, **insist** that the Pope in proper and full union with **HIS** bishops make the **AWESOME ECCLESIAL FATIMA CONSECRATION OF RUSSIA TO THE IMMACULATE HEART OF MARY.**

Chapter Eighteen

Will An Historical Paradox Save The World?

As we have seen and **proved**, the **prevailing forces** in Rome (and **thus,** in the Church) not only have disobeyed God's Fatima Commands, they have also **covered-up** their disobedience and even demanded that we perceive their GROSS SINS OF DIS-OBEDIENCE as being virtues. In effect, the spirit of New Age Catholicism prevails (at present) within Rome and within Christ's Church.

However, **paradoxically,** within the Russian Communistic dictatorship there seems to be developing "a moment of opportunity" -- an openness to prophecy, and specifically to the essential Fatima Message. As the Catholic Church seems to be rejecting, opposing and even condemning the Real Fatima Message or Prophecy, its God-rejecting enemy seems to be accepting and embracing the Spirit of Fatima. Let's consider these statements in greater detail.

New Age Catholicism Rejects And "Covers-Up" Fatima

The consecration "cover-up" has been programmed from Rome. Its execution is in the hands -- or, rather, the mouths -- of its "duped dopes."

"The evil one does not want the intercessory power of Mary's Heart known" - so advertises a priest spokesperson for the consecration "cover-up." According to him, Sister Lucia from March 25, 1984 on has continually said that "God will keep his word. The conditions are **now** [in 1990] fulfilled for the conversion of Russia."

You are being subjected to more confusion and more **lies** - especially regarding Sister Lucia (who on five occasions clearly and emphatically denied that Russia was properly consecrated on March 25, 1984, before she herself, was effectively silenced (or "imprisoned"), and became totally unavailable to **freely** express her true convictions. Just **what** does the Evil One gain from deceptions and lies regarding a consecration that **hasn't** been done?

He, Satan, The Father of Lies, will tolerate and even promote religion as long as it isn't true or "God-appointed" religion. Religion as such, isn't Satan's enemy - God's religion is.

New Age "Catholicism" is Satan's lie dwelling within God's sanctuary. "The smoke of Satan has entered God's sanctuary" - Pope Paul VI. Now, Satan is establishing the abomination of desolation in the sanctuary (Dan. 12:11) - New Age "Catholicism." MAN is taking God's proper place -- even within His sanctuary.

A few relevant characteristics of Satanic New Age "Catholicism" are: (1) the denial that the Catholic Church is the one true church of God - "extra ecclesiam nulla salus" becomes "outside of the church one can easily be saved;" (2) consequently, the denial, distortion or "watering down into meaninglessness" the truth that the Pope is the Supreme and only Head of the one true Church since he alone is the Vicar of Christ on earth; (3) the denial that the bishops are under the Pope and only have authority in as much as they agree with and are in union with the Pope and the real Catholic Church (as reiterated in Lumen Gentium of the Second Vatican Council); (4) the affirmation (in spirit, at least) that each church (Catholic or non-Catholic, diocesan or national) is autonomous and equally valid, (in effect, the belief that each religion or each dissenting national or regional episcopacy is as "good" as any other); and, (5) the denial and/or "watering down into meaninglessness" (the trashing and trivializing) of essential and relevant moral and doctrinal truths or doctrines, such as: the existence of real mortal sins (such as pre-marital sex, masturbation, drunkenness, adultery and gluttony), the existence of an eternally real Hell, the fact that Jesus and Our Lady of Fatima have disclosed that many go to Hell, the indissolubility of marriage, abortion as being murder, the existence of self-evident truth (real faith), the reliability of the Bible, the historical reliability of the Bible, etc.

Indeed, those who embrace Satanic New Age "Catholicism" cringe in fear as they are challenged to make the awesome Fatima affirmation of faith in the real and true Catholic Church. The real and true Catholic Church -- those who make up the Mystical Body of Christ -- are obedient to GOD'S WILL. This real and true Church is grateful for the FATIMA OPPORTUNITY and is eager to fully obey the FATIMA COMMAND regarding personal and ecclesial consecrations.

The awesome ecclesial Fatima Consecration is a profession of faith. Such a profession renounces all forms of New Age Catholicism. Such a profession of faith expels MAN from the sanctuary and tabernacle of CHRIST'S Church.

Man is reduced to a pitiful sinner who can only hope for salvation through obedience to God and His revelations, to Christ and to Christ's true church. Man is a pitiful sinner in need of

GRACE AND MERCY which he must receive from Christ's one and only Church. **Extra ecclessiam nulla salus.**

True Catholicism, not communism (communism with a small "c" which is embraced by many bishops and politicians in the "free world"), is the only hope of mankind. God, through Our Lady of Fatima demands that men bend their knees before Him. He demands that no god, even MAN - exist in place of Him.

God alone is our hope for salvation. Conforming to God's will as given at Fatima, is mankind's only hope for salvation - in the spiritual order as well as in the physical order.

Through the proper consecration of Russia, God will shower His graces upon us. Russia will be converted. The leaders of Russia, will no longer desire to spread the religion of Man (and thus the religion of Satan) throughout the world.

As Russia is converted and **RUSSIA'S ERRORS** are no longer promulgated, New Age "Catholicism" will lose its source of life. It will wither up and die.

Again, it's not that complicated. We must bend our knees to God, not MAN. We must humbly acknowledge that God is God and Man "ain't." We will then be led to make **reparation** for the past **outstanding** disobediences to the FATIMA GOD-GIVEN COMMANDS.

Satan is **the** Evil One. **Why**? He would **not** willingly bend his knee to God. The Pope and bishops join Satan - in as much as they refuse to conform to a rather simple, yet awesome God-given command regarding the consecration of Russia.

How do we know the command is God-given or prophetic? It **fulfils** the Biblical standards - those given by God. The command is Biblical (or in accord with the God of revelation) and **proven** to be from God (by the miracle of the sun and other prophecies that **were** fulfilled). See Chapter One - AUTHENTIC MARIAN PROPHECY.

GOD demands the consecration of **RUSSIA** (not of the world) by the Pope in union with the bishops of the world. **It's that simple. It's that awesome! It's that challenging!**

New Age "Catholicism" must be renounced - as the Devil is renounced at Baptism. Such "Catholicism" will be renounced by the one True Church when it **does** God's will as **demanded** at Fatima.

BUT, meanwhile, the establishment-Church seems to be worsening in its disobedience to, rejection of and "covering-up of" the Fatima Message. Can we look elsewhere for some sort of "breakthrough?" Can we look to Russia?

Is Russia Fatima's Hope?

At present (in 1991), the Catholic Church seems to consider FATIMA to be a (GOD-GIVEN) NUISANCE, EMBARRASS-MENT AND THREAT TO MANKIND. At present, there exists a **slight possibility** that Russia (its dictatorship) will come to see and embrace Fatima for what it really is -- **A GOD-GIVEN BLESSING FOR RUSSIA AND FOR THE WORLD.**

Will God "create" and use such an historical paradox -- that Russia which is the object of consecration come to demand its own consecration? Was Arnold Toynbee correct as he stated the following (in 1933)? **"Under the hammer and sickle as under the cross, Russia is still Holy Russia and Moscow the third Rome."**

Why is there such hope? In November of 1990, the Russian dictatorship published Alexander Solzhenitsyn's criticism of itself in its **Komosomolskaia Pravda** (with a circulation of about 25 million).

Such an act was equivalent to the American bishops (through their U.S.C.C., N.C.C.B. or national collections) underwriting, publishing and promoting **this book, The Wanderer, or Human Life International.**

On the whole, our Pope, bishops, etc. don't love prophetic truth nor do they have enough humility to confess and repent of their gross pastoral sins. However, do not the communists leaders seem to be operating with THE BEGINNINGS OF such dedication and humility?

Solzhenitsyn is "prophetic." As such, he embraces the spirit of Fatima. As such, he is a most vocal and strident critic of **RUSSIA'S ERRORS.**

Unlike those involved in the Fatima cover-up, he did not "repent of the truth." Instead, he **demanded** that Russia's leaders repent of their SINS in disobeying Truth.

Solzhenitsyn urged **"public acknowledgement of PARTY GUILT, of its crimes and its being a total failure."** In the true spirit of Fatima, he stated: **"in the past seventy years we have become so destitute, so devoid of life, so desperate that only Heaven can save us. BUT, Heaven's miracles do not come to those who are not humble enough TO BEG for them."**

As was proved in chapter two, reparation leads to consecration and is included in consecration. Reparation **demands** that we SINCERELY BEG FOR GOD'S BLESSINGS -- that we see our past SINS, confess them to God, acknowledge them before men, repent, make reparation and consecrate ourselves to Truth.

Wouldn't it be an "almost unbelievable paradox" that Russia's "atheistic leadership" would embrace the Fatima Spirit and then demand that the Pope obey God so that Russia could obtain God's blessings (if only for its material well being)?

Perhaps, Russia will "save Rome." Perhaps, Russia will be instrumental in leading Rome to discard its "reigning belief" that Fatima is **an embarrassment, nuisance and threat to mankind** and then to embrace Russia's conviction that **the awesome ecclesial Fatima consecration is a BLESSING "BEYOND BELIEF."**

Chapter Nineteen
The Pope And You
A. Don't Ignore The Pope And Bishops

Many, perhaps **most,** American Catholics embrace one of two positions with regard to the "Fatima" Consecration of RUSSIA. They are either "fed-up" with the Pope and the bishops, or they have a false and sinful loyalty to authority as it resides in the Pope and/or bishops.

These latter ones, we could say, sin by **adoring** the Pope and/or bishops. The former ones sin by **ignoring** the Pope and/or bishops. Our Lady of Fatima comes to free us from sin ... and to bring us to virtue.

Sin is avoided and virtue prospers by the proper approach or attitude towards consecrating Russia. Virtue is expressed and the cure (for these two sinful attitudes of ignoring or adoring the Pope as well as other sinful mindsets) is obtained and "applied" by one's proper attitude to the awesome challenge of consecrating Russia properly.

I have met quite a number of "Catholics" who have decided to ignore the Pope and bishops. Here are a few examples of their remarks.

Example 'A' --- "Our Lady has given up on Fatima. She now comes to Medjugorje.

She comes to the people since She failed in trying to 'straighten out' the church and its hierarchy. Only the people can be reached.

Forget about Fatima, it's 'past tense.' It failed. The clergy failed. The Catholic Church has failed miserably."

[These people have absolutely no evidence for their wild claims. They are creating their own "fantasy world" in order to avoid the awesome Fatima Challenges.]

Example 'B' --- "The church has re-defined itself since 'Vatican Two.' We have a new church -- a church of the people with priests and bishops as coordinators and facilitators.

No longer does 'the hierarchy' exist as it did before Vatican Two. They no longer have inherent authority from God, nor are they absolutely needed for us to get to God. They're only

elected by us in order to coordinate and facilitate the exercising of our individual charisma."

[These people are victims of APOSTASY WITHIN. They are opting for a Protestant Church -- not a Catholic Church.]

Example 'C' --- Some, especially Americans, demand simple and forthright answers or they'll ignore the associated challenge or problem. "Let Sister Lucia appear on television and clearly answer once and for all the question as to whether or not Russia has been consecrated properly." [During this period of the "cover-up," people seem to forget that Sister Lucia did this on at least five public occasions -- on each of these occasions, she simply and firmly assured us that Russia had not been consecrated properly, in 1984.]

[For these people, if Sister Lucia does not make a television appearance, when they demand one, they then choose to IGNORE the whole Fatima message, or, at least, the AWESOME FATIMA CONSECRATION.]

[These people also fail to understand Sister Lucia and her attitude. On the thirty-first of August, 1941, she confided her understanding of her mission to her Bishop : "Excellency ... I do not believe it was God's intention to present me to the world as a prophet." God wants His Church's pastors to embrace, propagate and properly respond to His Fatima Message.]

Reflection - The proper consecration of Russia will prove to Catholics and non-Catholics that the Pope is the Vicar of Christ on earth and that the Catholic Church (as "represented" by the bishops who are united with the Pope) is the one and only means of salvation (extra ecclesiam nulla salus). The Catholic Church is the one true Church of Christ - especially, in the Pope and then in the bishops united with him.

One ignores the Pope and the Catholic Church in its properly functioning bishops as united to the Pope, to his own peril. One is obliged to come to the one true church, founded by Christ.

B. Don't Adore The Pope and/or Bishops

I have met a sizeable number of Catholics who in their "apparently outstanding holiness," claimed that the Pope and bishops can't make a mistake. We must unite with their present mentality.

This is especially true in the present GLASNOST period (from the FALL of 1989 to the present and which will soon come to an end). **Apparently,** the Pope, Sister Lucia, the experts and "Rome" have all assured us that the consecration of Russia has been done and "done well."

"**Apparently**" is not "truthfully" or "convincingly!" There exists a cover-up and hoax of infinitely more importance than Watergate or Iran-Contra.

Shame on authorities who continue to take advantage of their positions to deceive the sheep. What will be **their** final punishment?

As was done previously, a few examples of such thinking will be presented. Along with the examples, I will give a correction or "refutation."

Example 'A' --- "The Pope is in charge of the church. He is Christ's Vicar on earth. It is disrespectful and scandalous to others to claim that he is wrong and that you are right. I'd rather agree with the Pope and disagree with you, rather than agree with you and disagree with the Pope."

Correction - Not everything the Pope says or does is infallible or emanates from his office as Head of the Church. **God** made him human. He has a free will and outside of his "official capacity," he can not only be deceived, he can also actively deceive.

He can not only do good, he can also do evil or sin. Such is reality! Liberals dogmatize the undogmatic and make the Pope infallible in areas where he is **fallible**.

Example 'B' --- "The Pope, Vatican officials, Sister Lucia and most of the experts assure us that the proper consecration of Russia has been accomplished. In such a case, it is only conducive to **scandal and disunity** to keep insisting that Russia be consecrated to the Immaculate Heart of Mary by the Pope, in union with the Catholic bishops of the world."

Correction - See chapter three on the consecration and its "cover-up." Realize that other "burials and cover-ups" have been employed in recent times. What happened to the Third Secret which was supposed to have been **disclosed** in 1960 (according to Our Lady's wishes) and then **acted on**? How can Rome fail to admit that the most important prayers of the Mass have been "protestantized?"

Why does the church pretend it has not **erred in practice** in so many areas - liturgy, catechetics, sacramental preparation, and the suppression of modernism, (to mention only a few areas)?

What about the ongoing "cover-up" by which the Church claims it believes in the indissolubility of marriage and yet is in the "wholesale" business of granting annulments in the U.S.A.?

Instead of "covering-up," why can't our hierarchy "**do reparation**" (as Our Lady of Fatima desires) which requires seeing and admitting **sins**, confessing them to God, ;"**repairing**" the damage done - by repentance, expressed by appropriate corrective actions - and sincerely determining or resolving to be watchful in the future so as not to allow such heresies, errors and evils to rise up again?

Conclusion: "In medio stat virtus." Don't ignore the Pope. Don't adore the Pope. Perceive and admit the truth about Fatima and about the Fatima cover-ups. Then, you are ready to do the right thing.

Work and pray. *Pray* **especially for the Pope - as Our Lady of Fatima told us to do. Also, as in any cause for which you have convictions -** *work* **to bring about the compliance by the Pope to** *God's command* **as given by Our Lady of Fatima.**

Why? The temporal and eternal, physical and spiritual well-being and prosperity not only of yourself and your "loved-ones" is AT RISK but the same well-being and prosperity of all others is AT RISK.

THIS is *your* **awful (full of awe and full of awfulness) challenge and opportunity -- YOU can** *pray and work* **to bring about the AWESOME CONSECRATION. You can become one with the holy children of Fatima -- one, in spirit and in truth. Regarding the Awesome Ecclesial Consecration Our Lady said, "Sacrifice yourself for this intention and pray".**

Perhaps, this is a good place to repeat Sister Lucy's words: "God will permit the grace of the consecration of Russia to Mary's Immaculate Heart when a sufficient number comply with the message of Fatima."

Chapter Twenty

Pope And Bishops Sinned And Still Sin

Quite a number of people expressed no difficulty with accepting Rev. Fr. Andrew Greeley's novel, THE CARDINAL SINS; yet, some refuse to admit that Pope and bishops not only sinned but still sin - especially as they continue to disobey God's command for proper ecclesial consecration of RUSSIA as given through or by Our Lady of Fatima.

Recently, I gave a talk to a Catholic group and happened to mention that the Pope and bishops had sinned in failing to obey God. A few were **shocked.** "How can **you** criticize the **Pope?** ... How can **you** condemn bishops?"

The **facts** are there. **God** commanded the Pope in union with the Catholic Bishops of the world to consecrate Russia to the Immaculate Heart of Mary. So far, the Pope hasn't obeyed God's Fatima Command.

As we have seen (chapter three, **THE GREAT "PAPAL VIC- TIMS" COVER-UP),** at least, **Pope** John the Twenty-third and subsequent Popes clearly have no excuse. They knew or know the Fatima Message.

Indeed, it is difficult for some of us to admit the awful and awesome truth that Popes sin (at least, materially). **Sin** is not **alien** to the human dimension, it is **natural** to it. **Therefore,** Sister Lucy has often told us: "PRAY FOR THE POPE!" Pray that the Pope may **soon** obey God's Fatima Commands.

Bishops also sin in as much as they disobey the God-given Fatima Commands. They sin by omission -- in as much as they fail to do **what God expects them to do regarding His Fatima Commands.**

To embrace the **mindset** that objective "Fatima-related" reality exists by which we can believe that man (even if he be a Pope or a bishop) sins, is, for evil people, to embrace an **alien** mindset. However, this "**alien**" mindset is the mindset of Fatima.

"**Many** living today will be in hell forever..." - Our Lady of Fatima. **Many!** In the words of little Jacinta: "Many many." Could not the **many** include a few (at least) bishops and perhaps even Popes?

We must be careful to avoid the **sinful** extreme as expressed in the unrealistic mindset that a Pope or a bishop **cannot** be sinful. The Pope -- in his official teachings -- is **infallible.** The Pope, **himself, is not** sinless! He too must pray: "Holy Mary, pray for me, a sinner, now and at the hour of my death."

To consider a Pope and/or bishop to be, in effect, sinless, is to "adore" Man as God and to build one's "house" on the sand of unreality.

Such a mindset is sinful. Such a mindset has prevented the Fatima Consecration, by encouraging the Pope and/or bishops to feel **sinless** in ignoring, dismissing and even lying about or "covering-up" Fatima's challenge.

People with this "anti-Fatima" mindset, see **nothing** that is correctable in the church. For them, apostasy cannot exist WITHIN the church - at least, among the "higher clergy." Yet, betrayal and gross sins among the higher clergy are deplored by the Fatima prophet, the **real** Sister Lucy.

No one should claim devotion to Our Lady of Fatima, if he, in effect, believes or holds as an operative mindset the "anti-Fatima" mindset which unrealistically and sinfully exalts the higher clergy as being, in effect, **sinless.**

Does not the Fatima consecration hoax or cover-up succeed by building on **this** anti-Fatima mindset? The **higher** clergy cannot deceive or be deceived according to the anti-Fatima creed.

Since the "FALL of 1989" some of the higher clergy "have orchestrated" the party line - that the consecration has been done and "well done" on March 25, 1984. These alleged "Fatima-ists" (who are vehemently against the real Fatima Message) are "**dogmatizing**" and propagating a lie as the truth. **They even present belief in their "Fatima-related" lies as a test of Catholic fidelity and unity.** Those who believe in these leaders are called upon to reject the truth and to hold a lie or a cover-up as being the truth.

Are such leaders sinless? Whom are they loyal to - God or Man? Whom have they betrayed - God or Man? In the name of God? In the name of the Pope? In the name of a Cardinal? In the name of the bishops? In the name of the experts? Or, is it in the name of sinning MAN, who happens to be a Pope, cardinal, bishop ... or even an expert?

Preserve your sanity. Preserve and strengthen your spiritual well-being. Renounce the anti-Fatima creed. Reject the worship of Man! Admit Popes and bishops have disobeyed God's command as given through Our Lady of Fatima.

Chapter Twenty-One

Deceive and/or Be Deceived -- In The Name Of God, The Church Or A Sinner ?

Will FACTS be enough to convince those who have an **over-whelming** devotion and allegiance to the **personages** of higher CHURCH OFFICIALS that a cover-up of the HIGHEST MAG-NITUDE has been perpetrated and continues to be perpetrated by the highest officials of the church? For some, yes; for some, no.

Some will be able to distinguish the reverence and obedience that they owe the office of a priest, cardinal or, even, a Pope from his fallible and sinful personage. Others won't be able to do this (largely and ultimately, because they are not "graced" to do so).

It was no different at the time of Christ. Christ told the people to respect the office of the Jewish priesthood, BUT, not to follow these priests - the scribes and pharisees - blindly and uncritically in what they said and did "unofficially" or as fallible and sinful individuals or as a fallible and sinful group (Mt. 23:2).

Indeed, the ability to understand and apply this Christ-given distinction might determine (or reflect) your eternal destiny - to be in Heaven or Hell forever. The Pope ... Cardinals X, Y, Z, ... Bishops L, M and N ... Fathers G, H and I ... and experts A, B and C tell us that Russia has been consecrated according to Our Lady of Fatima's specifications. How do you react?

What do the facts previous to the mega-cover-up indicate? In the Watergate cover-up, we didn't have previous facts before the cover-up. They were disclosed after the cover-up; yet, sensible people had no difficulty accepting the fact that evil officials existed.

However, we are blessed with the **previous facts.** Before the FALL of 1989, both the real Sister Lucy **and** the Pope acknowledged that **RUSSIA** was **not** consecrated as Our Lady desired on March 25, 1984. In **fact,** Sister Lucy stated this on **at least five public occasions** from 1984 or 1989. The Pope stated this **twice** on March 25, 1984 as he referred to: "those people who are still awaiting Our consecration."

Along with others, Malachi Martin, **the** expert on internal

Vatican affairs categorically denies that **RUSSIA** was consecrated on March 25, 1984. Yet, in spite of the **facts** - the testimonies of the real Sister Lucy and the Pope PREVIOUS TO THE SIXTH GLASNOST (the "fruit" of the Vatican-Moscow Marriage), some are foolish enough and rash enough to BELIEVE THE BIGGEST COVER-UP OF OUR CENTURY -- the continuing "FATIMA COVER-UP."

Conditioned To Time-Dependent Truth

Many of us are communists (communists with a small "c"). We are willing victims and even promoters of the Russian ploy by which "TRUTH" is determined by **contemporary state policy.**

Some higher officials in **the** Church are communistic - they too conceive and disseminate **time-dependent truth.** The "party-line" determines truth - that is, until the "party-line" is changed. For them, **contemporary church policy** determines "the truth." [This is clearly evident in the field of liturgical theory and practices.]

What's true this month may be false next month - dependent on the objectives of the ruling party. For example, Russia allowed easy divorces at one period of time and forbade them at another period of time.

MAN (the ruling experts or dictators) takes the place of GOD - and MAN is defined by the ruling party. **Morals** - what is right or wrong - are defined by the RULING PARTY (or, "the experts").

Those who are familiar with the works of St. Thomas Acquinas aren't surprised at this twentieth century "ecclesial-mega-sin." Bishop Fulton Sheen predicted that what St. Thomas taught -- that the last temptation to which the church would fall victim to would be for its clerics and hierarchy to become political (to put MAN before God and in the place of GOD) -- would happen in our present-day. The bishop punctuated his observations with the imperative: "WATCH IT!"

Indeed, Bishop Sheen and St. Thomas were perfectly correct. Unfortunately, we are the **victims** of the **great sin, the last sin -- the sinful ecclesial politicization of truth.**

Many examples of such politicizations occur today. One such happened in February of 1991. The Louisiana bishops issued a statement which promoted a state bill allowing murder by abortion in cases of rape, incest or danger to the life of the "mother."

Yet, **you** don't "**have to**" become a victim of sinful leadership. See the truth. Live in truth (as Our Lady said in the Ukraine in

1987). These are the end-times (as the real Sister Lucia assures us "from Mary" and as "Our Lady of the Ukraine" stated). These are the times of **nearly** overwhelming deception which Christ predicted (Mt.24).

See, live and pray so that **you** won't go to Hell forever. Realize that many have become victims of "Fatima-related lies" and other deceptions emanating from our church officials - either from them actively or by their passive consent as they **failed** to perform their **God-given duties** (especially, to witness to the truth at any cost).

Can Our Clergy Be Trusted?

Has not malfeasance in office and even betrayal "of" office occurred in areas such as the following (and have not many become VICTIMS) -- the practical and effective indissolubility of marriages; the Mass as Sacrifice and not as a mere meal; the teaching that not all are saved; the Catholic-community's witness that abortion is murder; the effective witness that Hell is real and many go there; and,the effective witness that certain sex sins are mortal sins which can bring one to an eternal Hell?

In each of the above mentioned areas as well as in many others, the higher clergy have not only failed to do their God-given duty; but, they have also deceived the faithful by effectively leading them to believe that wrong is right and that certain sins are not sins (in the real sense of the word, "sin").

"In the light of the present darkness," the Fatima "cover-up" is one more mega-cover-up, deception or lie. "Cover-ups" and "lies-propagated-as-dogmas" are COMMON to our sinful church leaders.

For example, we have been assured that the Third Secret would not interest us or that it is of "little significance for us." Yet, we are also assured from the context of Fatima, the real Sister Lucy and those who have read the Third Secret, that it pertains to such (insignificant?) things as: the loss of faith of whole continents, the gross corruption of the hierarchy, annihilation of nations, persecutions and executions, famines, floods, etc.

Can we trust the upper clergy?

Yet, even within our putrid spiritual atmosphere, the FATIMA COVER-UP stands out as one of the "most sinful" lies and betrayals of God which have ever occurred within God's church.

In view of the many prevailing lies, we must be careful to find the truth. We can only discover the truth by the help of

the Holy Spirit. As Jesus predicted, in these end-times, if possible, even the very elect of God would be deceived. Once we discover the truth, we must, by God's grace, never abandon it.

In spite of the many prevailing lies, we must work and pray that the proper ecclesial Fatima Consecration be done. We work and pray with absolute assurance of victory.

Mary assures us that a Pope will finally be freed from prevailing lies and the powers that propagate those lies. This Pope will put GOD before MAN and consecrate RUSSIA as God commands.

He will do it late - after mankind has suffered much, physically and spiritually. Then, the Immaculate Heart will triumph and a period of peace will be granted to the whole world.

To be sure, it is now LATE. Yet, it is never too late. Be sure you do what you can so that GOD'S will be done on earth.

Chapter Twenty-Two

What Is The Unity And Fidelity That We Should Seek?

The enemies of the real Fatima message preach "THE NEED OF UNITY IN THE CHURCH (from Fr. Robert Fox' ad in **The Wanderer, 9/10/90)**" as if it is an **absolute good.** Is UNITY an **absolute** good?

Would Fr. Fox and "like-thinkers" join the enemies of Jeremiah to **demand** that Jeremiah **unite** with the **majority** (the false prophets) or be murdered? Would Fr. Fox and "like-thinkers" join with the Egyptian N.C.C.B. (the National Bishops Conference) of the fourth century to depose and expel St. Athanasius since he refused to **unite** with the ecclesial **majority**?

Would Fr. Fox and "like-thinkers" join the **majority** of bishops in sixteenth century England to **demand** the conformity of the two or three "renegade bishops" who dared to claim that the Pope was Head of the true church?

Is **UNITY with and within the church establishment** our goal? Or, is **UNITY WITH TRUTH** our only goal?

UNITY is **not** an absolute good! **Today,** on certain issues (concerning which the apostate liberals are "in control") waving the flag of unity is an invitation to join the majority on their swift descent into further apostasy and an eternal Hell.

The **basic issue** is, and remains: Will you worship God on God's terms **or** will you "worship" Man on Man's terms, while neglecting or distorting God's Revelations?

A unity built on apostasy from God will bring you to Hell. A unity built on allegiance to God and apostasy from or INFIDELITY TO the controlling majority (in the religious and/or political realm) will, in our day and in **many** cases, bring you to an eternal Heaven. Take your choice as to which type of unity and fidelity that you prefer.

Don't believe in RED Russia. Don't believe in MAN. Don't reject God and God's revelations in order to please MAN.

Don't join the **apostates-within** and abandon Mary for the sake of "unity." Don't salute the liberal apostates' standard - the flag of UNITY. **One** with God; **one** with the real Mary is not only a majority, it is also the only UNITY worth embracing. **Think and pray about this!**

Chapter Twenty-Three

Help With The Fatima Ecclesial Consecration

Pope John Paul II would like to or "**wants to**" consecrate RUSSIA to the Immaculate Heart of Mary; but, he feels he "can't" do so. Why? He feels that he'll lose more than he'll gain.

Indeed, the Pope seems to be dedicated to Mary. He was involved in the consecration of Poland and the world to the Immaculate Heart of Mary and on March 25, 1984 as he consecrated **the world** in union with the bishops, he sadly remembered those "**people** who still await our consecration" - namely, the **Russian** people.

What does the Pope imagine or think he will lose by properly consecrating Russia? The support of some bishops - perhaps, some bishops will apostasize or go into (further) schism. He also fears for his very life, and, at least, for the "authentic life" of the Vatican since a pro-communistic (communism with a small "c") politico-religious force **now controls** a major segment of the Vatican itself.

How can **you** help solve the Pope's dilemma? 1) **Pray** for the Pope - as Our Lady of Fatima has urged us to do. 2) Urge the Pope **to do** what Our Lady of Fatima requested. 3) Urge your own bishop to favour and promote **the** Fatima ecclesial consecration. 4) Urge your pastor to do the same. 5) Support those "Fatima causes" which are true to Fatima and are effective. 6) Consecrate yourself to the Immaculate Heart of Mary (as suggested in part four). 7) Consecrate your "loved ones" to Mary.

Why do these things? The Pope, the bishops and all others within the "upper clergy" need **your** help: your "spiritually natural" help (through proper and effective pressuring of the upper clergy) and your "spiritual" help (by prayers and sacrifices).

We who are truly consecrated to Mary, work and pray with absolute assurance of victory. Therefore, rejoice and thank God for favouring **you** to be His special instrument, His Marian prophet. As such, be dedicated to doing all you can to obey **God's commands** as given to **us** through Our Lady of Fatima.

What is FATIMA? Let us review a few of the pertinent highlights of the Fatima Message. In 1917, Our Lady made six monthly apparitions to three little children (ages ten, nine and seven) at Fatima in Portugal.

Our Lady built Her message on the **PERSONAL CONVIC-
TION OF THE REALITIES OF SIN AND HELL.** She gave
these little children an "overwhelming experience" of Hell.

Why did She do this? Hell is the only and ultimate **eternal evil.**
Sin is the only and ultimate **temporal evil.** Hell is **the** consequence
of sin.

**THE PERSONAL CONVICTION OF THE REALITIES
OF SIN AND HELL** constitute the foundation upon which the
Fatima Message is built. Upon such a foundation, love for Jesus
and Mary (who are offended by SIN) and true love for oneself and
others become real and compelling (and for the great saints among
us as compelling as it was for the three seers of Fatima). **THIS
PERSONAL CONVICTION OF THE REALITIES OF SIN
AND HELL , by God's grace, can lead one to make and live the
awesome personal Fatima consecration -- a dedication of one's
whole life to Jesus through Mary or to Mary and thus to Jesus.**

**"Offer up to God all the sufferings He desires to send you in
reparation for the SINS by which He is offended, and in supplication for the conversion of SINNERS...Pray, pray very
much and make sacrifices for SINNERS, for MANY SOULS
go to Hell because they have nobody to pray and make sacrifices
for them " -- Our Lady of Fatima.**

Our Lady also assured us that **"Jesus wishes to establish in the
world devotion to My Immaculate Heart."** Such devotion or
consecration is to be both personal and ecclesial.

**"I shall come to ask for the consecration of RUSSIA to My
Immaculate Heart and the Communions of reparation...If My
requests are fulfilled, RUSSIA will be converted and there will
be peace. If not, RUSSIA will spread HER ERRORS
throughout the world promoting wars, persecution of the
Church, the good will be martyred...nations will be annihi-
lated... " -- Our Lady of Fatima.**

What was the requested ecclesial consecration? That the Pope
in union with all of the Catholic bishops of the world on one day
consecrate RUSSIA to the Immaculate Heart of Mary.

The Fatima Message demands the **awesome Fatima consecrations.** This is God's will. In this book we will consider the Fatima
Message, Challenge, Opportunity, Blessings and Consecrations as
well as our responses to them.

PART FOUR

YOUR AWESOME ACT OF CONSECRATION TO THE IMMACULATE HEART OF MARY

Introduction to Part Four

Indeed, the Marian Consecration Prayer or Act of Consecration to the Immaculate Heart of Mary is awesome. It concerns your eternal life.

If properly done and **lived**, it will bring **you** to eternal joy in Heaven. Also, on earth, as you die to your flesh and the world you will die **happily** or **blessedly** (as in the **eight beatitudes**), and you will live as you should.

Part four contains four chapters. First, the introduction presents ten major considerations which serve as a background for your personal consecration to the Immaculate Heart of Mary. Then, some pertinent FATIMA REFLECTIONS are given for you to pray about and "make your own" as convictions or abiding personal convicting awarenesses (PCAs).

Finally, three Consecration prayers will be presented -- a general one, a "weekly" one and a "daily" one. The general consecration prayer "comes from" the Pope's Marian consecration prayers of 1982 and 1984, as well as from Fatima's challenges.

The "weekly" consecration prayer (which can be prayed on Friday or Saturday of each week) is based on a meditative praying of the Five Sorrowful Mysteries of the Rosary (it is also the type of meditative praying that Our Lady of Fatima requested for the "five first Saturdays of Reparation"). The "daily" consecration prayer is a strong reminder of what it really means to be consecrated to the Immaculate Heart of Mary. All of these prayers express your **awesome personal Fatima consecration.**

Read and pray this part often. It is the "**personal heart**" of this book.

Chapter Twenty-Four

Introduction To Consecration

In order to properly and profitably consecrate yourself to the Immaculate Heart of Mary, pray about these ten major considerations (you also may wish to reconsider part two).

1. The message of Fatima was given by God through Our Lady of Fatima to help you to realize and "live-convinced" that **you** are a sinner by birth (original sin), by inclination (original and actual sin), in deed and in habit. Without Christ, **you** cannot be saved. You will go to Hell forever (provided, of course, you have reached the age of accountability).

2. The message of Fatima was given by God through Our Lady of Fatima to help you to realize and "live convinced" that **Hell** is the only and ultimate evil - the evil far worse...**indefinitely** worse than **you** could ever imagine it to be and the evil which lasts FOREVER.

3. The message of Fatima was given by God through Our Lady of Fatima, to help you to realize and "live convinced" that **Hell** is possible for **you**. "Many living today will be in Hell forever" - Our Lady of Fatima. Unrepented or insufficiently repented mortal sin will bring **you** to an eternal Hell.

4. Therefore, Our Lady of Fatima wants you to realize and "live convinced" that **the** goal of your life is to save your soul from the eternal torments of Hell.

5. Also, **living in true charity**, you are to "live convinced" that what "hurts" God, the Sacred Heart and the Immaculate Heart are SINS. **You** can make reparation to God, Jesus and Mary for your sins and the sins of others.

You can save souls (and their bodies) from eternal Hell by your prayers and sacrifices (Col. 1:24). **You** can save yourself and others. You can "console" Jesus and Mary. Here is **charity, true charity!**

6. HOW do you "conquer" your "natural" state of estrangement from God or your "**natural**" tendency to live in SIN, even mortal sin? (The **real** Council of Trent solemnly stated that one cannot live without falling into mortal sin without the special help of

God*).You conquer your "natural" state by CONSECRATION in word and in deed.

7. Christ is THE CONSECRATOR. He is the One and Only One through, with and in whom you can become holy, sanctified or just (acceptable to God). He sanctified Mary and through Mary, He can sanctify you.

8. Christ offers you the New and Eternal Covenant in His Blood (which is "re-presented" at each Mass in an "unbloody" manner). Through this Covenant Christ is among us - Christ wishes to dwell in you, to bring you into **Holy Communion with Him**: NOW, in time; and, FOREVER, "in eternity."

He wants you to come to live, not you, but Him in you (Gal.2:20). He wants you to accept Him fully - to be consecrated to Him so as to be transformed (Rom. 12:2) and to live, not you, but Christ in you (Gal. 2:20).

9. In these end-times, **especially,** Christ wants your consecration to be to the Immaculate Heart of Mary and **thus** to Him **or** to Him through the Immaculate Heart of Mary.

Only in this way will you receive GRACE AND MERCY **to live as consecrated** and to be restored to such living should you "fall into sin." Indeed, GRACE AND MERCY was the initial message of the angel of Fatima and the message in the last great revelation at Tuy (the vision of the "Trinity Crucifixion and The Immaculate Heart of Mary at the Mass altar of sacrifice and Holy Communion").

10. Do **you** want to freely and fully consecrate yourself to the Immaculate Heart of Mary [to desire to become (and to become) holy "with" or by Christ through Mary]? Remember, consecration is **a lifetime sacrifice** - making **(facere)** holy **(sacrum)** - accomplished by the mysterious combination of God's grace and **your** free will.

Before you consecrate yourself to the Immaculate Heart of Mary, reflect on some pertinent messages from Fatima. Reflect on these selected messages in the light of the ten observations we have just made.

These selected messages emanate from Fatima. Become totally convinced that they are **personally relevant God-given truth.** Meditate on these words from Fatima - from Jesus Christ, the Blessed Virgin Mary, the angel of Fatima and the real Sister Lucy **THE** Marian Seer of our day.

* "If anyone says that **without God's special help** it is possible for a justified man to persevere in the justice he has received, or says that with God's special help it is impossible; let him be Anathema. (Cannon 22 of the Decree on Justification... The Council Of Trent).

Chapter Twenty-Five

Fatima Reflections

There follows selected Fatima reflections. Let these come alive for you:

A. Hell Exists As A Real Possibility

SIN is the only and ultimate evil. Why? Unrepented or insufficiently repented mortal sin will bring any and every human being to **ETERNAL HELL.**

"You have seen Hell where the souls of poor sinners go. In order to save them, God wishes to establish in the world, devotion to My Immaculate Heart. If what I say to you is done, many souls will be saved..." - Our Lady of Fatima.

The Fatima Vision Of Hell:

"Our Lady opened Her hands once more, as She had done during the two previous months. The rays of light seemed to penetrate the earth, and we saw as it were an ocean of fire.

Plunged in this fire were demons and souls in human form, like transparent burning embers, all blackened or burnished bronze, floating about in the conflagration, now raised into the air by the flames that issued from within themselves together with great clouds of smoke, now falling back on every side like sparks in a huge fire, without weight or equilibrium, and amid shrieks and groans of pain and despair, which horrified us and made us tremble with fear. The demons could be distinguished by their terrifying and repellent likeness to frightful and unknown animals, all black and transparent.

This vision lasted only a moment, thanks to our good Heavenly Mother who, at the first apparition, had promised to take us to Heaven. Without this promise, I think we would have died of fright."

Our Lady recalls to us so insistently: "Many are those who are lost and at the end of their life of sin they fall into this 'ocean of fire' which is Hell."

"More souls go to Hell for sins of the flesh than for any other sins" - Our Lady of Fatima.

"Many marriages are not good; they do not please Our Lord and are not of God" - Our Lady of Fatima.

Lucy relates to us her conversation with Jacinta: "'Jacinta, what are you thinking of?' Jacinta replied, 'About the war which will come. So many people will die, and almost all of them will go to Hell.'"

It is of utmost importance that each of us examine his **FUNDAMENTAL ASSUMPTION**. Is it in line with the Fatima Message? Is it in line with God's Word?

Do you believe **many** will go to Hell? Do you believe that only a few will go to Hell? Consequently, do you believe that you have only a very slight or absolutely no chance of going to Hell; or, that you have a chance of going to Hell?

Sister Lucia clearly and forcefully reassured Fr. Lombardi (Feb. 7, 1954) that **MANY**, not a few, would go to Hell forever. Little Jacinta, in her childlike way, also assured us that "**MANY MANY**" would go to the eternal Hell.

B. Be Consecrated To Mary

"You have seen hell, where the souls of poor sinners go. To save them, God wishes to establish in the world, devotion to My Immaculate Heart" - Our Lady of Fatima.

"To those who will embrace this devotion to My Immaculate Heart, I promise salvation" - Our Lady of Fatima.

Jacinta said to me: "**Tell everybody that God grants us graces through the Immaculate Heart of Mary, that people are to ask Her for them; and that the Heart of Jesus wants the Immaculate Heart of Mary to be venerated at His side. Tell them also to pray to the Immaculate Heart of Mary for peace, since God has entrusted it to Her.**"

Our Lady of Fatima promised Lucy: "**You will never be alone. My Immaculate Heart will be your refuge and the way which will lead you to God.**"

Sister Lucy reports what Our Lord Himself said: "**I desire most ardently, He says, the propagation of the cult of the devotion to the Immaculate Heart of Mary, because the love of this Heart attracts souls to Me; it is the center from which the rays of My light and My love go through all the earth, and the unquenchable fountain from which the living water of My mercy flows into the earth.**"

Our Lord told Sister Lucy: "**See, My daughter, the motive for which the Immaculate Heart of Mary inspired Me to ask for this little reparation, and in consideration of it, to move My mercy to pardon souls who have had the misfortune of offend-**

ing Her. As for you, always seek by your prayers and sacrifices to move My mercy to pity of these poor souls."

Sister Lucy explained to Father Fuentes: "The holy Rosary and devotion to the Immaculate Heart of Mary are our two last recourses, and so this means there will be no others...With a certain trepidation God offers us the final means of salvation, His Most Holy Mother."

C. How Do You Live This Consecration To The Immaculate Heart Of Mary?

In general, live a life of prayer, obedience, mortification and conversion (come to faith or grow in faith). This is the awesome Fatima challenge.

When the Blessed Virgin told her that soon she would leave for the hospital and that she would suffer much there, Jacinta said to her cousin: "'...I'll be there suffering all alone! I'll suffer for love of Our Lord, to make reparation to the Immaculate Heart of Mary, for the conversion of sinners and for the Holy Father.'"

"I found Jacinta joyful as ever, glad to suffer for the love of Our Good God and of the Immaculate Heart of Mary, for sinners and the Holy Father. That was her ideal, and she could speak of nothing else."

"'Don't be afraid,' she told Lucy, 'in Heaven I'll be praying hard for you, for the Holy Father, and for all priests.'"

At Tuy, Our Lady discloses the following fact: "So numerous are the souls which the justice of God condemns for sins committed against Me that I come to ask for reparation. Sacrifice yourself for this intention and pray."

Our Lady of Fatima gave us this awful warning and command: "They must not continue to offend Our Lord, Who is already deeply offended....Pray the Rosary every day to obtain peace for the world....Pray, pray a great deal, and make sacrifices for sinners, for many souls to go to Hell because they have no one to make sacrifices and pray for them....Jesus said, "THE SACRIFICE I COMMAND OF EACH PERSON IS THE ACCOMPLISHMENT OF HIS OWN DUTY AND THE OBSERVANCE OF MY LAW."

"Jacinta would often sit on the ground or on a rock, and she would say, growing pensive: 'Oh, hell, hell! How sorry I am for the souls that go to hell! And the people who are there, being burned alive, like wood in a fire!' And she would kneel down, half trembling, with her hands joined, to recite the prayer Our Lady had taught us: 'Oh my Jesus, forgive us, deliver us from the fire of hell, lead all souls to Heaven, especially those who are most in need'... And Jacinta would remain kneeling for a long time, repeating the same prayer."

Then, Sister Lucy asks: "How is it that Jacinta, small as she was, let herself be possessed by such a spirit of penance and mortification, and understood it so well?"

"I think the reason is this: first, God willed to bestow on her a special grace, through the Immaculate Heart of Mary; and secondly, it was because she had looked upon hell, and had seen the ruin of souls who fall therein."

Sister Lucy asked Francisco: "'Francisco, which do you like better: to console Our Lord, or to convert sinners, so that no more souls go to Hell?'

'I would rather console Our Lord. Didn't you notice how sad Our Lady was that last month, when She said that people must not offend Our Lord any more, for He is already much offended? I would like to console Our Lord, and after that, convert sinners, so that they won't offend Him any more.'"

Lucy recalled about Jacinta: "At times, she kissed and embraced a crucifix, exclaiming: 'Oh my Jesus! I love You, and I want to suffer very much for love of You!'

"How often did she say: 'Oh Jesus! Now you can convert many sinners, because this is really a big sacrifice!'"

D. A Special Way To Be Consecrated

Jesus told Sister Lucy: "Have compassion on the Heart of your Most Holy Mother, covered with thorns, with which ungrateful men pierce It at every moment, and there is no one to make an act of reparation to remove them."

Then the Most Holy Virgin said: "Look My daughter, at My Heart, surrounded with thorns with which ungrateful men pierce Me at every moment by their blasphemies and ingratitude. You at least try to console Me and announce in My name that I promise to assist at the moment of death, with all the graces necessary for salvation, all those who, on the first Saturday of five consecutive months shall confess, receive Holy Communion, recite five decades of the Rosary, and keep Me company for fifteen minutes while meditating on the fifteen mysteries of the Rosary, with the intention of making reparation to Me."

Sister Lucy gave the following PEACE PLEDGE FORMULA:

Dear Queen and Mother, who promised at Fatima to convert Russia and bring peace to all mankind, in reparation to Your Immaculate Heart for my sins and the sins of the whole world, I solemnly promise:

1) To offer up every day the sacrifices demanded by my daily duty; 2) To say part of the Rosary (five decades) daily while meditating on the mysteries; 3) To wear the Scapular of Mount Carmel as a profession of this promise and as an act of consecration to You. I shall renew this promise often, especially in moments of temptation."

E. The World And Some Members Of The Church Become Ever More Demonic. Our Consecration Becomes More Difficult And More Urgent:

Sister Lucy in responding to a militantly orthodox priest states: "There is a diabolical disorientation invading the world and misleading souls! It is necessary to stand up to it; ... and, staying in my place, I pray for you and for all those who work with you.

Sister Lucy deplores the fact that so many pastors: "let themselves to be dominated by the diabolical wave invading the world," and are "blind men leading other blind men."

"THE BLESSED VIRGIN KNEW THAT THESE TIMES OF DIABOLICAL DISORIENTATION HAD TO COME."

Sister Lucy reiterates her observation that we live in a time of extreme rottenness on the part of many people within the Church and within society: "Foreseeing this [present] disorientation, the Virgin recommended recitation of the Rosary with such insistence as 'the prayer most apt for preserving faith in souls.' It is because She already knew that these times had to come, when the devil and his supporters would fight so much...She armed us against this time of diabolic disorientation ... and false doctrines."

Sister Lucy deplores the great success that the devil is enjoying in our day. She also reminds us that the AWESOME FATIMA CONSECRATIONS can defeat him: "The devil has succeeded in infiltrating evil under cover of good, and the blind are beginning to guide others as the Lord tells us in His Gospel, and souls are letting themselves be deceived.

Gladly I sacrifice myself for priests and for all consecrated souls, especially for those who are so deceived and misled!"

"This is why the devil has waged such a war against it! And the worst is that he has succeeded in leading into error and deceiving souls having a heavy responsibility through the place which they occupy ...! They are blind men guiding other blind men..."

NOTE: All of the above quotes were taken from the three volume works of Frere Michel de la Sainte Trinité - THE WHOLE TRUTH ABOUT FATIMA - which can be obtained from THE FATIMA CRUSADER, 452 Kraft Road, Fort Erie, Ontario. L2A 4M7 or THE SERVANTS OF JESUS AND MARY, R.D. #1, Box 258, Constable, N.Y., 12926.

Chapter Twenty-Six

The General Marian Consecration Prayer

[The following Act of Consecration to the Immaculate Heart of Mary is based on the 1982 and 1984 acts of consecration by Pope John Paul II (at Fatima and in Rome), as well as on the apparitions at Fatima].

I fly to Your protection, O Holy Mother of God.

My Mother, Mary, You know my sufferings and my joys, my sins and my virtues, my true love and my lack of love. You console me and win for me, graces to conquer daily temptations. Without the graces You give to me from Your Son, I will fail.

I now offer and consecrate to You, to Your Immaculate Heart, my entire being. Through You, I consecrate myself - and am consecrated to - the Sacred and Adorable Heart of Jesus, Your Son, my God and Savior, my Lord and my All.

I consecrate myself to You to "console" Jesus and You for the many sins committed against God. Especially will I "pray the Mass" and receive Holy Communion in reparation for my sins and the sins of others which grieve so much Your Immaculate Heart and the Sacred Heart of Jesus. I will also pray Rosaries for the same intention as well as for the conversion and salvation of sinners.

I put myself under - and am put under - Your mantle. When I fail, do not, I pray, reject my prayers. Accept them as I remain ever desirous to be truly consecrated to You and thus to Christ, Who is our one and only Consecrator.

Indeed, Christ is our Consecrator. Without Him, we are nothing. Through Him, we are sanctified and consecrated: "And for them do I sanctify (consecrate) Myself, so that they may be consecrated (sanctified) in truth (Jn. 17:19)." Through Christ will I become who I should be - now and forever.

The love of Christ for us is so strong that He allows us to share in His role as Consecrator. We can, by our Christian sacrifices and sufferings, add something to the sufferings of Christ for the sake of His Body which is the Church (cf. 2 Cor. 12,15; Col. 1:24). We can be crucified with Christ for God's glory and for the salvation and sanctification of ourselves and others.

The love of Christ is without bounds for You, His Mother, the one and only sinless human person. Christ, Your Son, loved You so much that He made You The Mediatrix and Fountain of all graces. He is the Source. You are the Fountain. As Your special child by my act "and life" of consecration, remember me in my **true** needs which can only be satisfied by God's merciful graces.

I deeply need to be consecrated to You and thus to Your Son. From Your Son, through You, will come the GRACE AND MERCY, THE LOVING KINDNESS OF GOD, which I so desperately need in order to come to You in Heaven and to avoid eternal misery in Hell.

As Your special child, grant that I may always be saddened by and "uncomfortable with" anything that is opposed to holiness and consecration. Grant that I may have "more than sufficient" graces to return to You and Your Son, should I commit a mortal sin.

As Your special child, help me to imitate You in Your detestation of SIN as the only and ultimate evil and in Your total and perfect obedience to God, for it is only in obeying Christ's Covenant that I am consecrated to Christ through You. Help me to empty myself out in obedience to the Covenant and the Wishes of God (Phil. 2:4-8; Lk. 1:38) and **thus** to come closer to You who are defined as **SINLESS.**

Let me never neglect coming to the New and Eternal Covenant in the Blood of Christ - the Mass - for through this unbloody sacrifice of Christ, Your Son, I am made a partaker of the divinity of Christ; I am prepared for Heaven - the eternal adoration of the Lamb Who was slain (Apoc. 5:6-13); and, I am given even now the Pledge and Foretaste of Heaven - "the adoration of the Lamb Who was once slain" and the Body, Blood, Soul and Divinity of Christ, Your Son, in Holy Communion.

Grant that my appreciation of and participation in Mass as well as receiving Holy Communion may make me ever more sensitive to Sin and bring me to a greater detestation of SIN for SIN is the only and ultimate present evil.

Grant that I may love as You loved. Grant that I may love God totally and exclusively.

Then, **in** and **through** that love, grant that I, like You, may go out to others in true and perfect charity - caring for their eternal destiny, as You care for the eternal salvation of souls -- mine and those of others.

Grant that I may with true contrition and purpose of amendment, not only see and confess my sins, but come to comprehend more and more the great mystery of sin (2 Th. 2:7), which is the only and ultimate present or temporal evil.

Grant that I may comprehend (as best I can be graced to com-

144

prehend) the horror of **sin** by coming to realize -- as Your special children of Fatima realized -- the extreme indescribable and unimaginable horror of **Hell.** Hell is the eternal result of dying with even one unrepented or insufficiently repented mortal sin on one's soul. Help **me** to firmly and continually believe this great "Christ-revealed" dogma of the Catholic Church.

Therefore, please grant to me Your child by consecration, to love . God, Jesus, Yourself, myself and others as I should - according to Christ's Covenant Decrees. Thus, grant me the grace to avoid sin, especially mortal sin which could put **me** in Hell forever.

Help me no longer to live for or "from" my sinful flesh (Rom. 8:1-13; Rom. 13:14; 1 Peter 3:21; 2 Peter 2:10; 1 Jn. 2:16). Help me no longer to live for or "from" this sinful world system (2 Cor. 4:4; Gal. 1:4; Jas. 4:4; Hb. 11:6).

Help me to live by faith (Rom. 1:17; Rom. 14:23; Lk. 18:8; Hb. 11:6). Help me to be renewed and transformed in heart and mind (Rom. 12:1-4). Finally, grant that I may come to live, **not I,** but Christ in me (Gal. 2:20).

Grant all of these tremendous graces and mercies of God through my consecration to You and thus to Jesus. Despise not my petitions; but, in my **necessity** hear and answer me O clement, O loving, O sweet Virgin Mary, my Mother and the Mother of our God and Savior, Jesus Christ.

Lastly, in the special prophetic and "end-times'" light of Your FATIMA MESSAGE, I consecrate myself - desire to and strive to be made and become HOLY **with** and by God's grace and mercy in Christ Jesus as attained through You, by You and in Your Immaculate Heart.

As consecrated to You, I am and will be devoted to the Saving Mystery and Saving Presence which is the Mass and Eucharist. I join Your very special children of Fatima in their great love of the Mass and Eucharist.

As consecrated to You, I wish to become ever more sensitive to and convinced about SIN as being the only and uttermost present evil and about HELL being the unimaginably uttermost ETERNAL Horror and Punishment which is the effect of dying in the state of having even one unrepented or insufficiently repented mortal sin "on one's soul."

Grant me the grace, O Blessed Mother, to live with this **abiding** personal convicting awareness (this abiding PCA), FOR ONLY THEN will I be able to join the very special children of Fatima in their desire and continual firm resolution to pray, obey, convert, (grow in faith) sacrifice and mortify myself so that: (1) I can save my own soul (and specially recreated body) from the **eternal** pains of Hell, (2) I can save others from Hell: (3) I can console and make reparation to the Sacred Heart of Jesus and Your Immaculate Heart.

Grant me, also, Our Lady of Fatima, to pray the special prayers of Fatima often and fervently:

"O my Jesus, forgive us our sins, deliver us from the fires of Hell, lead all souls to Heaven especially those in greatest need (of your graces)" - the prayer given by Our Lady of Fatima.

"My God, I believe, I adore, I hope and I love You! I ask pardon for those who do not believe, do not adore, do not hope and do not love You" - The Angel of **Peace**.

"Most Holy Trinity, Father, Son and Holy Spirit, I offer You the most precious Body, Blood, Soul and Divinity of the same Son, Jesus Christ, present in all the tabernacles of the world, in reparation for the sacrileges, outrages and indifference by which He Himself is offended. And through the infinite merits of His Most Sacred Heart, and the Immaculate Heart of Mary, I beg of You, the conversion of poor sinners" - The Angel of the **Eucharist.**

Grant me a special devotion to the Rosary. Help me to say it every day. Help me also to make the "First Five Saturdays" as You desire them to be made. Help me to make them as often as possible. Thus, also, will I grow in my practice of receiving the Sacrament of God's grace and mercy.

Holy Mary, Immaculate Virgin, Mother of God, my Mother, Our Lady of the Rosary, Our Lady of Fatima, pray for me, a sinner, now and at the hour of my death, Amen.

Chapter Twenty-Seven

A Weekly Consecration Prayer

Once a week -- on Friday, recalling the redemptive sufferings of Christ, or on Saturday, recalling Our Lady, or on Sunday, the Lord's day -- either prayerfully contemplate the following "mysteries" by themselves, or prayerfully contemplate them as "mysteries" ATTACHED TO your praying five decades of the Rosary.

Preliminary Prayer:

I consecrate myself to the Immaculate Heart of Mary and thus to the Sacred Heart of Jesus. In doing so, I give my life to Jesus through Mary, or to Mary and thus to Jesus (since Mary is Immaculate and perfectly divinely feminine and thus **totally** lovable by God).

I consecrate myself in the "light of" these five mysteries. I consecrate myself in order to console Jesus and Mary by making reparation for my sins and the sins of others -- realizing or striving to be graced to realize that **SIN IS THE ONLY AND ULTIMATE PRESENT EVIL (just as Hell is the only and ultimate eternal evil)**. I also consecrate myself for the salvation and sanctification of my soul and the souls of others **especially:..(mention those you wish to pray for)........**

I. THE DIVINE FEET OF JESUS -- Your divine, yet human, feet teach me to go and to be **WHERE** You want me to go and/or to be. Your divine feet -- from Your Conception on -- were totally obedient to the Father's will. Your divine feet won for me the graces to go and to be **WHERE** You want me to go and to be.

Help me, then, to perceive and to remove: all selfish ambition, laziness, discontent, anger and the like -- which not only sour my consecration to You, but which are **SINS**. Positively, teach me and "grace me" (and help me) to be virtuously industrious for the accomplishment of Your will in my life -- especially, concerning the **WHERE** of my life.

II. THE FLESH WOUNDS OF JESUS --Your adorable Body suffered much during Your lifetime, especially, at the Scourging. Your Body was and is **sacramental.** Your Body tells me **HOW I** am to live even as I am given graces by Your sufferings to live as

I should.

May I always be, or may I become, convinced that my flesh (my brain and my body) and the world (the natural, unredeemed or unsanctified communities of men -- ecclesial and social) are my **enemies**. They can bring me to an eternal Hell. May I be graced to mortify my flesh and to despise the world.

Grace me, especially, O Lord Jesus, to see **HOW** I am living for my flesh and this world. By Your sufferings and by the "**compassionate**" sufferings of Your Mother, Mary, grant me the graces not only to perceive my sins; but also, to eradicate them.

Grace me to live **crucified with You**. Grace me to live **crucified to my flesh and to this world**.

III. THE DIVINE HANDS OF JESUS -- Your divine, yet human, hands teach me and "grace me" to **DO** what You want during my brief life on earth. From the beginning of Your human life, Your adorable hands did God the Father's will -- as an example for me and to give me the grace to **DO** as You desire and thus to be saved from Hell and be with You for all eternity in Heaven.

Grant me, O Lord Jesus, the grace to be content and industrious in **DOING** Your will -- beginning with the Ten Commandments to **DOING** each of my daily duties as You desire. I need your graces to **DO** Your will.

I thank You for Your graces. In a special way, I thank you for Your graces which have allowed me to **DO** Your will and **thus** to live freed from: fear, worry, frustrating self-ambitioning, jealousy, unresolvable regrets and similar "fruits" which come from living for/from this world and/or my flesh.

IV. THE CROWN OF THORNS -- Your skull was pierced with thorns. In this way, You "graced me" and taught me to **THINK** as You desire. I am to have or to come to have every thought subject to You (II Cor. 10:5).

"Grace me" to **THINK** as You desire -- to be aware of **my actual thinking** and then to confess my sinful **THINKING** as well as my helplessness without Your grace in not **THINKING** as I should. Help me to cooperate with Your graces so as to come to **THINK** as You desire. I also thank You for Your graces of the past and Your present graces which lead me to desire or "to possess" this great blessing.

V. THE PIERCED HEART -- Your adorable human Sacred Heart was pierced for me. Thus, You "graced me" and taught me

148

to **DESIRE only** God and God's will.

I now recall the great Fatima Vision at Tuy. In this vision, You taught us many great truths. In this vision, You confirmed the great truth that **sin** is the only and greatest present evil; and, that **LOVING KINDNESS** or **GRACE AND MERCY** come from You through Your Mother, Mary, and through the Holy Sacrifice of the Mass and Holy Communion. In Your own way, You save us from **sin and Hell.**

Help me to **live my consecration.** Help me to **DESIRE** only what You want. Help me to come to You through my consecration to Mary.

Help me, dear Jesus, to come to **DESIRE** as the only perfect human person, Mary, desired. Help me to live consecrated to Mary -- **DESIRING** to do only God's will. Help me to **DESIRE** and **TO LOVE** You totally and exclusively. **Then, I will be living my consecration perfectly.**

Chapter Twenty-Eight

"Daily" Meditation Prayer For My Awesome Personal Fatima Consecration

By God's grace, I consecrate myself to the Immaculate Heart of Mary. She alone is totally and perfectly open to being done to as God wills and CONSEQUENTLY to doing as God wills.

Through God's graces "won" for me by Christ and given to me through the Immaculate Heart of Mary, I will strive to live with "the heart of Mary." As much as I can, by God's grace, I resolve to give myself, in the power of the Holy Spirit, to God the Father through Christ and Mary -- to be done to and to do as God the Father desires.

With and through Mary, I join Christ in His sacrificial life. Through Christ, in the power of the Holy Spirit, my flesh (my brain and body) is given up to God the Father to be done to as the Father desires; and, the chalice of my blood (my will, deeds and ambitions) is given up to God the Father "to do" or "to be" as the Father desires. As it were, by living my consecration to the Immaculate Heart of Mary, my flesh and my blood become the flesh and blood of Christ -- as I live, not I, but Christ in me.

As consecrated, my whole life is dedicated to "being done in memory of Christ" -- obedient to His will (as revealed in my conscience, the Bible and the real Catholic Church). THUS, my unique eternal life will be an eternal thanksgiving with and through Mary in Christ to God the Father in the power and grace of the Holy Spirit. May my eternal life be the eternal fruition of the Lamb that was slain in perfect obedience to God the Father's will.

[If possible, say this prayer at Mass.]

PART FIVE

FATIMA'S AWESOME AFFIRMATIONS

Chapter Twenty-Nine

Affirmations and Denials

This chapter expresses the AWESOME consecrations by giving a series of what these consecrations - personal and ecclesial - AFFIRM and DENY. These affirmations and denials clearly and forcefully illustrate why the Fatima consecrations are AWESOME. **Meditate on these affirmations and denials.**

Lastly, you will notice that **most** of these "couplets" refer to the awesomeness of the **ecclesial** consecration. However, remember personal consecrations both reflect and lead to the ecclesial one -- Our Lady of Fatima promised that when a sufficient number have made and are living their **awesome personal consecrations to the Immaculate Heart of Mary,** then such an outpouring of graces will be granted to our ecclesial leaders that the **awesome ecclesial consecration of Russia to the Immaculate Heart of Mary** will be made.

Finally, by reading and meditating on these "couplets," you will become convinced of the meaning and necessity of making the **awesome Fatima consecrations.** Then, you will "naturally" be industrious in leading others to make these consecrations so that they may receive God's blessings.

Each Awesome Fatima Consecration:

Affirms -- GOD is GOD

DENIES -- MAN IS GOD

Affirms -- The only and ultimate evil is SIN and its eternal result, HELL.

DENIES -- TEMPORAL AND/OR PHYSICAL EVILS ARE THE EVILS.

Affirms -- My only life goal is to save and sanctify my soul and to save the souls of others from HELL and thus to give comfort to Jesus and Mary.

DENIES -- LIFE IS MEANINGLESS OR IT IS TO BE DEFINED IN TERMS WHICH EXCLUDE GOD AND/OR GOD'S RELATIONS, ESPECIALLY AS GIVEN TO IN THE BIBLE AND IN THE PROVEN PROPHECY OF FATIMA. DENIES -- SOULS DO NOT EXIST. DENIES -- ETERNAL LIFE IS NOT IMPOR-

TANT. DENIES -- THE MOST WE CAN BELIEVE IN IS REIN-CARNATION.

Affirms -- Christ through Mary is My Bridegroom and the Bridegroom of Christ's Church. Like Mary, I am the slave of God, and of Christ.

DENIES -- MAN THROUGH ANY WORLD LEADER OR GROUP OF WORLD LEADERS IS MY LORD AND MY ENSLAVER.

Affirms -- Eternal Dimension is THE dimension.

DENIES -- EARTH DIMENSION IS THE DIMENSION.

Affirms -- That our Mass Prayer versions in the Novus Ordo have taken a wrong direction (towards man and away from God). Also, that there are many other ecclesial abuses and evils in our churches which must be addressed and eliminated.

DENIES -- NOVUS ORDO (SAECULORUM) MASSES ARE THE BEST, AND OTHER "GOD-DENYING" OR "GOD-WEAKING" CHANGES ARE BETTER OR EVEN GOOD, AS SUCH.

Affirms -- God is free to command as He desires in these end-times - by focusing on Mary.

DENIES -- REVELATION AND GOD ARE TO BE UNDER-STOOD BY HOW THE "EXPERTS" OR "AUTHORITIES" TELL US TO INTERPRET OR UNDERSTAND THEM.

Affirms -- My sinful past and the need for me to "make reparation" for the past as I confess my sins and resolve to live as God desires - especially as spelled out by the entire authentic Fatima Message.

DENIES -- I'M NOT SINFUL. I DO THE BEST I CAN. GOD LOVES ME JUST AS I AM.

Affirms -- The primary role of the Immaculate Heart of Mary in these end-times is to bring us to Jesus, God and Saviour.

DENIES - DEVOTION TO THE IMMACULATE HEART OF MARY IS, AT LEAST, TOO EMBARRASSING FOR MODERN MAN AND, AT BEST, SHOULD BE QUESTIONED AND DENIED.

Affirms -- Our sinfulness and utter inability by ourselves to cope with living in these horrible and dangerous end-times. We need to be consecrated to Mary.

DENIES -- I AND OTHERS ARE CONTENT AND LOOK FORWARD TO THE GREAT MAN-MADE UTOPIA WHICH IS ABOUT TO COME: FOR SOCIETY AND FOR THE CHURCH.

Affirms -- Man needs Religion as God defines it.

DENIES -- MAN DEFINES GOD AND RELIGION AS HE THINKS BEST.

Affirms -- The so-called Protestant Reformation was really **THE PROTESTANT REVOLT** or major apostasy.   At Fatima, God reiterates that the Catholic Church is the one and only true church of Christ. The Pope is of utmost importance -- for Catholics and for all mankind. The fate of the one true Church and, THUS, of the world are in HIS HANDS.

Beliefs that were attacked or denied by the Protestant Revolt or Great Apostasy as well as by New Age Catholicism and the prevailing "spirit of ecumenism" are reaffirmed and underlined at Fatima. Examples of such are: we are not saved by a "once and for all Protestant type of belief" but by faith expressed in a LIVED CONSECRATION; the Mass and the Eucharist are indeed what the Catholic Church has always believed them to be; the Bible, like Fatima, is not open to subjective interpretation or "subjective belief and twisting," but is objective and clearly understood; and, devotion to the Mass and the seven Sacraments, devotion to Mary and to the Rosary are of utmost importance, especially, in these end-times.

DENIES -- THE PROTESTANT REVOLT WAS GOOD. WE, CATHOLICS, NEED TO CONTINUE THE PROTESTANT REFORMATION BY BECOMING MORE PROTESTANT, ESPECIALLY, IN OUR MASS PRAYERS AND MORAL TEACHINGS. DENIES -- THE "SPIRIT OF VATICAN TWO" WHICH LEADS US TO BELIEVE THAT ONE RELIGION IS AS GOOD AS ANY OTHER AND THAT IF YOU DO WHAT YOU THINK IS RIGHT, YOU WILL GO TO HEAVEN.

Affirms -- True love of mankind is to obey God and, especially, to live the Fatima Message.

DENIES -- CONTEMPORARY "CHARITY" WHICH CLAIMS

TO LOVE MAN FOR HIS OWN SAKE AND WHICH CLAIMS WHATEVER MAN DECIDES (APART FROM GOD'S REVELATIONS) IS GOOD, JUST AND HOLY.

Affirms -- The infinite value of each of us. As a sufficient number obey God as He spoke in proven prophecy at Fatima - they not only save their own souls, but they, together, can, as it were, bring down from Heaven, sufficient grace to change ecclesial disobedience into obedience. They can help "save" their sinful hierarchy and thus the Church and the world.

DENIES -- THE HIERARCHY IS IMPECCABLE, THAT THEY CANNOT SIN, THAT WHATEVER THEY DO IS RIGHT JUST BECAUSE THEY CHOOSE TO DO IT THAT WAY. DENIES -- THAT EXACTLY AS THE HIERARCHY SEES FATIMA IS THE WAY FATIMA IS. DENIES -- THAT THOSE MEMBERS OF THE HIERARCHY ARE RIGHT WHEN THEY IN FACT SEE ANY ASPECT OF RELIGION IN A WAY THAT DOES NOT CONFORM TO THE TRUTH.

Affirms -- Our primary unity is to be with God and to obey God's commands as given to us through His Revealed Will.

DENIES -- GOD'S REVEALED WILL ISN'T CLEAR OR CON-TRADICTS ITSELF. THEREFORE WE ARE LEFT TO FOL-LOW "(CHURCH AND STATE) EXPERTS AND DICTATORS." THUS, OUR ONLY UNITY MUST BE SUPER-FICIAL AND/OR MAN-MADE - DEFINED BY MEN AND IMPOSED UPON US BY MEN.

Affirms -- Man needs Redemption and God's special graces in these end-times.

DENIES -- MAN IS SELF-SUFFICIENT. MAN - THE EX-PERTS AND AUTHORITIES - DON'T NEED GOD'S HELP IN THESE END-TIMES. THEREFORE, I DON'T NEED GOD'S HELP.

Affirms -- YOU, by "believing in," promoting and supporting the ecclesial and personal consecrations, put GOD in first place.

DENIES -- MAN - YOURSELF OR THE COMMUNITY - IS YOUR PRIMARY CONCERN (AND, THUS, YOUR GOD).

Affirms -- YOU love God first and foremost, totally and ex-clusively. Then, you relate to or care for others "in the light of" or "for" the love of God.

DENIES -- MAN - YOURSELF AND/OR THE COMMUNITY - IS TO BE LOVED AND CARED FOR, NOT AS GOD DIRECTS, BUT AS "ENLIGHTENED" MEN (ESPECIALLY "THE EXPERTS," AUTHORITIES AND REIGNING CHURCH AND STATE POWERS) DECIDE, DECLARE AND "DOGMATICALLY DECREE."

Affirms -- Man is born to attain - by free will and God's grace - Heaven.

DENIES -- MAN IS FROM/FOR THIS EARTH; OR, MAN CAN "NATURALLY" REINCARNATE OR EVOLVE INTO PERFECTION.

Affirms -- Man, because of his fallen state, is "naturally" sinful.

DENIES -- MAN IS GOOD OR NEUTRAL.

Affirms -- Man needs salvation from God (by God's grace).

DENIES -- MAN CAN PERFECT HIMSELF.

Affirms -- Man needs to make reparation for his sins.

DENIES -- REPARATION IS NO LONGER NEEDED. MAN IS FREE FROM SUPERSTITIOUS AND/OR CONFINING RELIGIOUS SYSTEMS AND CONCEPTS SUCH AS SIN, HELL AND LAWS FROM "ON HIGH."

Affirms -- Man's only hope is in consecration to Christ (through consecration to Mary). Why? He is not sacred and needs to be "sacred-tized" by being "set apart with Jesus," or "secrated con Jesus."

DENIES -- MAN'S HOPE IS MAN.

Affirms -- American Constitution in its original and true meaning is good.

DENIES -- THE PRESENT DISTORTED AND LYING INTERPRETATION OF THIS CONSTITUTION IS CORRECT OR RIGHT.

Affirms -- All forms of socialism are sinful.

DENIES -- ALL FORMS OF SOCIALISM ARE GOOD.

Affirms - Power of prayer and consecration to Mary.

DENIES -- POWER OF MAN AND THE NEED TO THINK AND

157

WORK TO CREATE UTOPIA **A LA CHARDIN** [A FUTURE CREATED BY MEN ("THE EXPERTS") AND FOR MEN (THE ENSLAVED)].

Affirms -- The individual is endowed with inalienable rights, responsibilities, dignity and freedom.

DENIES -- THE INDIVIDUAL IS PART OF THE STATE OR OF "THE COMMUNITY" AND HAS THE RIGHTS AND FREEDOM THAT THE MEN-CONTROLLED STATE OR "COMMUNITY" GIVE TO HIM.

Affirms -- History is God's story or His story. God is supreme and truly Catholic Reconstructionism is our only hope.

DENIES -- CURRENTLY POPULAR EVOLUTION-UTOPIA RELIGION. MAN COMES FROM NATURE OR CHANCE. MAN IS TO BE EVOLVED **A LA CHARDIN** OR BY THE WILL OF **"THE EXPERTS"** AND DICTATORS WHO, ALONE, ARE ABLE TO DIRECT OUR PROPER EVOLUTION WITHIN THE "NUOSPHERE."

Affirms -- Russia's system and similar ones are ERRONEOUS and DEMONIC.

DENIES -- OUR HOPE IS IN **SOCIALISM** OR SMALL "C" COMMUNISM (SUCH AS: SOCIALISM, "CATHOLIC SOCIALISM," SECULAR HUMANISM AND THE NEW AGE).

Affirms -- Power of Mary. She through the graces of God, converts Russia. She conquers Russia's errors.

DENIES -- SMALL "C" COMMUNISM IS DESIRABLE. WE ARE **HELPLESS** AND **MUST** BECOME MORE AND MORE SOCIALISTIC.

Affirms -- Popes and bishops (collectively and thus individually) have sinned in the past. Why? When they finally obey God as they consecrate Russia as God commanded through Our Lady of Fatima, demonstrating that they did not obey before.

DENIES -- POPES AND BISHOPS EITHER CONSECRATED RUSSIA PROPERLY IN THE **PAST** AND WERE GOOD ECCLESIASTICS **OR** IN NOT CONSECRATING RUSSIA AND IN IGNORING FATIMA THEY WERE GOOD AND JUST.

Affirms - Popes and bishops have sinned. They need to make

reparation for their sins - which brought eternal and/or temporal misery not only to themselves and to "their" church; but also, to all of mankind.

DENIES -- POPE AND BISHOPS CAN DO AS THEY PLEASE AND ALWAYS BE RIGHT IN ECCLESIAL MATTERS.

Affirms -- Popes, bishops and higher clergymen have "grossly sinned" by issuing, propagating, imposing and "dogmatizing" COVER-UPS OF THE TRUTH. These wicked clergymen have not only denied and disobeyed the truths of Fatima -- THEY also have "dogmatically decreed" that their disobedience is to be seen as and to be proclaimed to be OBEDIENCE.

DENIES -- WHATEVER OUR CHURCH OFFICIALS DO IS RIGHT. WE SHOULD NOT QUESTION THEIR ACTIONS OR DECISIONS. THEY ARE IN THE PLACE OF GOD AND MUST BE OBEYED. THEY CAN NEITHER DECEIVE OR BE DECEIVED. THE ESTABLISHMENT IS SINLESS.

Affirms -- Catholics have *betrayed* Christ and need to "right their wrongs" or to return to God, to Christ and to the true Church. The "protestantizing and secularizing" of the Church was a HORRIBLE SIN.

DENIES -- PROTESTANT REFORMATION WAS A REFORM. THE PROTESTANTIZING AND SUBSEQUENT SECULARIZING OF THE CATHOLIC CHURCH (IN PRACTICE, ESPECIALLY IN "THE WEST") IS DESIRABLE AND BENEFICIAL.

Affirms -- Guilt and the diabolic disorientation of the upper clergy. They sinned in not obeying God by properly consecrating Russia. They continue to sin by being subject to diabolic disorientation - as Sister Lucy has pointed out.

DENIES -- THE UPPER CLERGY SEE THE TRUTH AND DO WHAT'S RIGHT. THEY CANNOT BE SUBJECT TO DEMONIC DELUSIONS.

Affirms -- SIN is in an age which is blind to SIN.

DENIES -- GOD ACCEPTS US AS WE ARE -- THERE IS NO SIN OR WE ARE SINLESS.

Affirms -- Fatima - essentially and historically - shows forth the mysterious relationship between God's grace and man's free will.

DENIES -- THERE EXISTS NO SUCH THING AS THE MYSTERY OF GRACE/FREE WILL.   GRACE IS TO BE TRIVIALIZED AND DENIED.   ALSO, MAN'S FREE WILL (ESPECIALLY, AS BEING ACCOUNTABLE TO GOD) SHOULD BE TRIVIALIZED AND "HORIZONTALIZED" (DEFINED ONLY IN TERMS OF **THIS** WORLD).

Affirms -- Hierarchical and priestly nature of the Church and thus the importance and reverence due each priest - in his office and in his person. The priestly office will be "priortorized" and protected from lay take-over. Thus, the dignity of each priest is restored and protected.

DENIES -- LAY EMPOWERMENT OR TAKE-OVER OF THE PRIESTLY OFFICE - PREACHING, DISTRIBUTING HOLY COMMUNION, ETC. NO REAL AND PRACTICAL RESPECT IS TO BE SHOWN TO THE PRIESTLY OFFICE AND THUS TO THE PRIEST. THE BISHOP'S LIBERAL "MACHINERY" EMPOWERS LAY PEOPLE - **NOT** THE LOCAL PRIEST. HE HAS **NO** DIGNITY OR RIGHTS - HE IS SUBJECT TO THE LIBERAL "MACHINERY." THE PRIEST IS THERE TO COORDINATE AND FACILITATE THE FUNCTIONING OF THE CHARISMS OF THE LAITY ACCORDING TO THE EDICTS OF THE BUREAUCRACY.

Affirms -- The Pope is the Vicar of God, the Vicar of the Church and the Vicar of all mankind. As he obeys God, we prosper. As he disobeys God, we suffer.

DENIES -- THE UNIQUE ROLE OF THE POPE IS A FICTION OF THE PAST AND NO LONGER EXISTS. THE NEW CHURCH, FORMED BY VATICAN TWO, REALIZES THAT BISHOPS, NOT THE POPE, RUN THE CHURCH.

Affirms -- We are saved - both spiritually and physically - by complying with (that which appears to us in our wickedness as) God's totally arbitrary will (for example, His command given to us at Fatima that we are to make the awesome Fatima consecrations).

DENIES -- GOD - IF HE EXISTS - CAN ONLY COMMAND AS

WE, THE "EXPERTS" DECIDE (AT LEAST, GOD MUST ACT WITHIN OUR DEFINED PARAMETERS). THEREFORE, WE, THE REIGNING FATIMA EXPERTS AND AUTHORITIES, HAVE DECIDED, DECREED AND "DOGMATIZED" THAT THE FATIMA MESSAGE CAN IN NO WAY BE GOD'S DEMAND; AND, THAT THE FATIMA MESSAGE (FOR WHAT IT'S WORTH) HAS BEEN COMPLIED WITH BY THE POPE AND BISHOPS. THEREFORE, YOU, OUR SUBJECTS, MUST IGNORE FATIMA'S DEMANDS AND BELIEVE THAT RUSSIA WAS CONSECRATED PROPERLY IN 1984. IF YOU DON'T BELIEVE THIS, YOU ARE WORKING AGAINST FIDELITY AND UNITY.

Affirms -- Our nation, and our world, are under God with proper and true liberty, justice and freedom with responsibility for all, according to God's Revelation.

DENIES -- OUR NATION, AND OUR WORLD ARE UNDER MEN (THE "EXPERTS" AND TYRANTS) WITH MAN-DEFINED LIBERTY, JUSTICE AND FREEDOM FOR ALL IN VARYING DEGREES AND WAYS AS MEN (THE EXPERTS AND TYRANTS) DECIDE.

Affirms -- Catholic Church is THE means of salvation. Extra ecclesiam nulla salus, outside of the church there is no salvation.

DENIES -- THE FALSE ECUMENICAL SPIRIT PREVALENT SINCE THE SECOND VATICAN COUNCIL. ONE RELIGION IS AS GOOD AS ANY OTHER, PROVIDED, OF COURSE, EACH APPROVED RELIGION THINKS THIS IS TRUE.

Affirms -- A Radical Annulment and full divorce has been granted to the Vatican Moscow marriage.

DENIES -- THE VATICAN - MOSCOW AGREEMENT AND SUBSEQUENT MARRIAGE IS GOOD FOR THE CHURCH AND MANKIND AND OUR HOPE FOR THE FUTURE.

Affirms -- Russia's errors and gross evils (communism and its deeds) are to be exposed, acknowledged as such and condemned as such. The Russian people are dedicated and consecrated to the Immaculate Heart of Mary. They are set apart by the Pope and HIS Catholic bishops as united with him, for God's special blessings: that they may be converted to the One and Only

161

True Church, the Catholic Church. Russia, AS A POLITI-CAL AND SOCIAL ENTITY, is consecrated to the Immaculate Heart of Mary so that it will be converted to the truth. Russia, AS A POLITICAL AND SOCIAL ENTITY, will no longer exist as a communistic nation. Russia's errors will no longer be propagated throughout the world. The world will be returned to peace with Christ. How? Through the Fatima consecration of Russia to the Immaculate Heart of Mary. INDEED, THE ECCLESIAL FATIMA CONSECRATION IS AWESOME!

Chapter Thirty

Conclusion: You Are Responsible The Choice Is Yours

SINCE WE -- A SUFFICIENT NUMBER OF INDIVIDUALS -- HAVE FAILED TO MAKE AND LIVE THE AWESOME FATIMA CONSECRATIONS, MANKIND HAS SUFFERED AND WILL INCREASINGLY SUFFER SUCH EVILS AS THE FOLLOWING:

**** MANY souls have gone to an eternal Hell and many more will go to an eternal Hell.

**** Russian Communism has flourished and is subjugating people to its tyranical dictatorship. In establishing itself, Communism has murdered more than 100,000,000 individuals. It continues to murder those who won't submit to its godless dictatorships.

**** Russia's errors continue to spread throughout the world as small "c" communism is imposed upon free God-loving people. The U.S.A., South America and Canada are becoming increasingly small "c" communistic.

**** Small "c" communism is taking over our land while SIN AND SIN'S EFFECTS continually increase in the form of: apostasy and heresy within American Catholicism; rejection of God and God's Revelation as contained in the true Catholic Church and the real Bible; family breakdown finalized in divorces and unwarranted annulments; the promotion of and imposed favoring of homosexuals, welfare "leeches" and other individuals with sinful life-styles; abortion; violence; drug-abuse; etc. etc. ad nauseam. Increasingly, we turn from God to man; and, increasingly, we force others to turn from God to man as our civilization self-destructs.

****Various nations have been destroyed and will be destroyed. Wars and persecutions of the truly faithful will increase and intensify.

Yet, You Are Responsible.
The Choice Is Yours.

If You:
(1) OBEY THE FATIMA MESSAGE.

(2) MAKE AND LIVE THE AWESOME PERSONAL FATIMA CONSECRATION.

(3) DO ALL YOU CAN TO BRING ABOUT THE AWESOME ECCLESIAL FATIMA CONSECRATION OF RUSSIA TO THE IMMACULATE HEART OF MARY.

Then:
{ 1 } "IF MY REQUESTS ARE GRANTED, RUSSIA WILL BE CONVERTED AND THERE WILL BE A PERIOD OF PEACE GRANTED TO THE WORLD" --- OUR LADY OF FATIMA.

{ 2 } "IF PEOPLE DO WHAT I TELL YOU, MANY SOULS WILL BE SAVED" --- OUR LADY OF FATIMA.

{ 3 } OF INFINITE AND ETERNAL IMPORTANCE TO YOU, YOU WILL BE SAVED FROM THE FIRES OF HELL AND BE WITH JESUS AND MARY FOREVER IN THE ETERNAL JOYS OF HEAVEN.

An Epilogue:

My Personal Reflections And Conjectures Concerning The End-Times' Significance Of The Fatima Revelations

I contend that the Fatima Revelations are totally biblical and relevant to our day. I will focus on the actual and "projected" responses to or attitudes towards Fatima -- especially, by Popes (and, in particular, Pope John Paul II).

Read this epilogue with an open mind. Hopefully, it will ultimately lead you to **intensely live the AWESOME FATIMA CONSECRATION** in the realization of its **AWESOME END-TIMES BIBLICAL SIGNIFICANCE** for yourself, for the Church and for the world. Remember, these are my own personal conjectures and reflections.

[A] Non-Papal And Papal Predictive Prophecies Concerning Our End-times

Prophecy is speaking forth God's truth in a relevant manner. This can be done "predictively" or "presently." Either way, true prophecy tends to elicit a God-given "ouch" or "amen."

Blessed Anna Emmerich, a stigmatist in the nineteenth century, saw in a vision: "...the Church of St. Peter in ruins...**many** excommunicated clergy, unconcerned and even unaware of their being excommunicated [since, as she correctly observed, they "embraced opinions to which an anathema had been attached"]...the Catholic religion fell into complete decadence as **everything pertaining to Protestantism gained the upper hand.**" It would seem that she wrote this in Chicago yesterday, instead of in Germany in 1820.

We have several other "non-papal" predictions from the past which concern our times. For example, in 1634, Mother Mary Torres in Quito, Ecuador saw that for a large part of the twentieth century "various **heresies** will flourish on this earth."

What is **heresy**? "Heresy is the obstinate post-baptismal denial or **doubt** of some truth which must be believed with **Catholic** or Divine Faith (Revised Code of Canon Law, no. 751)." (In the U. S. A., surveys conclusively prove that **most** "Catholics" disagree with one or more **essential Catholic truths.**)

Mother Mary Torres tells **us** that to escape from these heresies "will call for great strength of will, constant courage and great trust in God -- all of which come from the merciful love of Christ."

Perhaps, in the near future, we will even be called upon to heed **Saint** Catherine of Sienna's grave warnings. She told us that a Pope who falsifies his function will go to Hell; and, furthermore, that those who obey him will go there with him.

Why do I cite Saint Catherine? Mother Mary also predicted about our present day: "the devil will take glory in feeding perfidiously on the hearts of children. The innocence of childhood will almost disappear. **Thus,** priestly vocations will be lost, it will be a real disaster. Priests will abandon their sacred duties and will depart from the path marked out for them by God. **Then,** the Church will go through a dark night for lack of a **Prelate and Father** to watch over it with love, gentleness, strength and prudence, and numbers of priests will lose the spirit of God, thus placing their souls in great danger."

In our own day, Sister Lucy, the remaining seer of Fatima, confirms the fact that we are living in horribly dangerous end-times."The Most Holy Virgin made me understand that we are living in the last times of the world. She told me that the devil is in the process of engaging in a decisive battle against the Blessed Virgin Mary, the **final** battle...Either we are for God or we are for the devil. There exists no other possibility."

A Few Papal Predictions

On October **13th,** [the same month and day of the final public apparition at Fatima], 1884, Pope Leo XIII experienced a vision in which he perceived that God's graces would be lessened and Satan would wreck havoc **WITHIN THE CHURCH** for the next hundred or so years.

At the beginning of the twentieth century, Pope Saint Pius X was "terrified by...the disease -- apostasy from God (E Supremi Apostolatus Cathedra, Oct. 4, 1903)."

He prophetically perceived this internal apostasy as "the **foretaste and the beginning of those evils reserved for the last days**...In very truth, we cannot think otherwise in virtue of the audacity and wrath employed everywhere in persecuting religion, in combatting the dogmas of faith, in the firm determination of up-rooting and destroying all relations between man and God...**this** is the distinguishing mark of The Antichirst -- **with unlimited**

166

boldness man puts himself in the place of God....He sits in the temple of God as if he were God...**(E Supremi, #5)**."

As it were, the "infant heretics" whom **Saint** Pius X condemned became the "adult **periti**" of the pastoral and "non-dogmatic" Second Vatican Council. Worse yet, the same heresies which Pope Saint Pius X condemned and prophetically predicted would "rise again," **now** are preached from the very sanctuaries of Christ's church.

These heresies and others flourish within New Age Catholicsm which is the religion of antichrist and, as such, the forerunner; or, prominent part of, (or even the very essence of) the Second Beast of the Apocalypse (as we shall show later on).

This **is** the age which Pope Pius XII, Pope Paul VI and Pope John Paul II have all characterized as the age that has LOST A SENSE OF SIN. We have sold out to the devil.

Pope Paul VI perceived the devil's smoke **within** God's sanctuary -- so much has Satan advanced within God's church. In many places, Satan, as it were, has taken God's throne (as was predicted by Saint Pius X). Satan dwells **within** the very sanctuary of the existential church.

The present pontiff, Pope John Paul II, perhaps more than anyone else, realizes that we are now in the awesome end-times. When questioned by German bishops as Fulda, November, 1980, concerning our times and the Fatima "secret," the Pope "predicted" what Mary already promised (in the second Revelation of Fatima) -- that **horrible** sufferings and persecutions unto death are in store for mankind.

"We must be strong. We must prepare ourselves. We must entrust ourselves to Christ and His Holy Mother and we must be attentive, very attentive, to the prayer of the Rosary" -- Pope John Paul II in response to the German bishops.

[The official Vatican paper reacted as if the above-mentioned dialogue never occurred. Here we have one more "cover-up" of the embarrassing and unpleasant truth.]

Also, at the beginning of his pontificate the Pope said: "We are in the days of the **final** confrontation between the gospel and the anti-gospel and between the church and the antichrist."

"Awesomely and unfortunately," the Pope still refuses to obey the Fatima Command. Instead, he seems to be intent on pleasing, or even "worshipping," MAN, not God, as he strives to form or "greatly inform" the New World Government of man by man -- **without** obedience to God and His Revelation (ultimately, the First Beast of the Apocalypse). As we shall see, in supporting, promoting and forming the First Beast, the Pope puts himself in danger of becoming the Second Beast -- pray for the Pope!

[B] Fatima's Three Apocalyptic Revelations

Sister Lucy and Cardinal Ratzinger have read the Third "Secret." They both refer us to the Apocalypse -- chapters eight through thirteen.

All three REVELATIONS of Fatima (which because of the prevailing influence of papal **disobedience,** we commonly refer to as "secrets") are **biblical.** Our Lady of Fatima has come to tell us that the bible is being fulfilled in our day -- "**NOW IS THE APOCALYPSE.**" We are **now** in apocalyptic times -- the end-times.

I. The First Fatima Revelation

Pope John Paul II realized this **fact** as he boldly stated: "**We are living in the final confrontation** between Church and antichrist and between the gospel and the antigospel."

Our Mother came to earth in 1917 to remind us of "church and gospel." Through the true Church **and** the true Gospel comes salvation.

Our Lady reaffirmed "**Catholic basics**" -- which are questioned, doubted, trivialized or, even, denied in present day Catholicism. A few of these **basics** are as follows.

Each soul is under a test. Each of us will go to and abide within an eternal Heaven or an eternal Hell. Realizing even to some slight extent, the horrible evil of Hell is God's grace to us. It was Mary's special GIFT to Her chosen loved-ones -- the seers of Fatima.

Our world and our "individual-flesh" lead us into Hell -- not Heaven. We must pray, sacrifice and obey God in order to be able to avoid Hell and to go to Heaven.

Lastly, each of us can participate in the great "Pauline mystery" -- being "co-redeemers" of others (Col. 1:24). Somehow, our prayers and sacrifices can save others from eternal Hell.

The first Fatima Revelation re-emphasizes these and other basics of our faith. **This** is extremely relevant as we live within churches which no longer have faith or transmit the true faith. Our "faith-less" leaders and experts have attacked and destroyed the

Catholic understanding of, appreciation of and proper "use of" basic Catholic "entities" such as: the Bible, the Mass, catechesis, morals, dogmas, the nature of the church, etc.

We thank Our Lady for the First Revelation. We consecrate ourselves to Her and **thus** to Jesus so that we **can** live as we should in these incomprehensibly dangerous end-times.

II. The Second Fatima Revelation

Russian "God-less" cruelty and **Russian errors** will be used by God to punish us for our sinfulness. The only hope that each of us has is to make and to live the Fatima Consecration.

As a sufficient number of us live consecrated lives, Russia will be consecrated by the Pope together with his bishops on one particular day to the Immaculate Heart of Mary (this day will also be a day of REPARATION).

The Second Revelation, I contend, takes us into a specific part of the Bible -- Apoc. 12:17 to 13:10. Here is the First Beast.

This First Beast (according to the rules of biblical language) is **a type of government**. It is **Russian errors** (in the language of Fatima) which includes any and all types of government which are similar to Russian government -- secular humanism, mitigated or New Age Communism, New Age or One World government, socialism, murderous communistic dictatorships, and the like. In general, **Russia's errors or Russian errors** is that type of government which makes **man** central and which ignores or opposes God and God's will for man.

Russia's errors is New Age Political Government -- at least, **nascently.** This Baby Beast (when it "evolves") will become the First Beast of the Apocalypse and will obtain its power from Satan as it continues to join him in disobeying God and glorifying MAN (whose number is 6 -- on the **sixth** day, man was made).

This Beast will bring with it wars, the annihilation of nations, great sufferings for the just, etc. Already, **everywhere** that Communism has been imposed **millions** of people have suffered and died. For example, millions were **murdered** after the Communists took over Vietnam.

It is difficult in 1991 to realize that Russia is still God's instrument for chastising us for our **sins**. Russia seems to be suffering from a mortal wound.

Yet, "its mortal wound was healed and the whole earth followed the Beast in admiration and wonder (Apoc. 13:3)." Russia even as it suffers "a mortal wound" remains the most powerful nation in the world. Imagine what it will be when "it recovers."

The Second Revelation also assures us that RUSSIA'S (OR, THE FIRST BEAST'S) ERRORS will spread throughout the world. As Solzhenitsyn observed, we in America are **voluntarily** Communistic.

(For example, we are presently engaged in eradicating God-given morality as we legislate to allow murder by abortion and to give those who live in the unnaturally sinful lifestyle of "sodomizing" a privileged status. Also, we are now in the process of transferring parental **rights** over their own children to state-control under the guise of "imposing" the U.N.'s "Rights of the Child" legislation.)

Our legislatures and judges increasingly presume and mandate a "God-less" and "faith-less" government. Russia's (the First Beast's) errors are becoming our "truth." Russia's errors are spreading throughout the world -- especially, within the U. S. A. Indeed, the First Beast -- New Age, Russian or Communistic type of government -- is not only alive but is conquering the world. World socialist leaders, led by West German Will Brandt, proclaimed at a conference in 1991 that world socialism has never been stronger (see *The McAlvany Intelligence Advisor*).

Worst of all, because we ignore Fatima, we don't even perceive the ever worsening problem. Eventually, the piper will be paid.

Eventually, we will suffer horrible afflictions for our **sins** -- as foretold by Our Lady of Fatima in the Second Revelation.

We will suffer. The just will be persecuted and murdered. Blood will flow throughout our nation from the "very fact" that we have embraced and imposed Russia's (or, the First Beast's) ERRORS upon American citizens.

Why is this happening? We have failed to perceive, to listen to and to obey the Fatima Message. "The Holy Virgin is very sad because nobody is concerned about Her Message -- the good as little as the evil" -- Sister Lucy of Fatima.

"Russia will be the Scourge chosen by Heaven to chastise the entire world if we do not obtain its conversion" -- the real Sister Lucy. The Pope must properly consecrate Russia -- otherwise, Russia and Russia's ERRORS will devastate our world.

Demonic prophets within our Church (in 1991) assure us that **Russia** is being converted -- yet, the number of **Catholics** in Russia is less than 70,000. Is **that** the conversion of a nation of over 200 million?

How stupid can these prophets be? How stupid must they presume us to be?

III. The Third Revelation Of Fatima

"I saw a **Second Beast** rise out of the earth. It had two 'horns' like a LAMB, but it spoke like a dragon. It exercises authority with the First Beast and makes the earth and its people to worship the First Beast whose mortal wound was healed. It works great signs, even making fire come down from heaven... it deceives those who dwell on earth... it slew those who would not worship the image of the Beast... the number of the Beast is the number of MAN (Apoc. 13: 11-18, my version)."

The **First Beast is the rule or government of man by man according to man's "God-less" standards. The Second Beast is the "SOUL" of the First Beast.**

The **Second Beast is like a LAMB. It resembles God's true Church, within which dwells the LAMB OF GOD. Yet, it has the "SOUL" or spirit of Satan, the dragon.**

There's a great and fundamental principle at work here. **Russia's errors** (which Our Lady of Fatima tells us will spread throughout the world) are based on a fundamental principle which it shares with the **Second** Beast (within which New Age Catholicism is "a" or "the" prominent part).

This fundamental principle **in recent times** was born in Protestantism -- MAN is the measure or Judge of just what God says or doesn't say. MAN is above God. In effect, **MAN is God.**

The **first** Bible discussion group is alive and well -- "Did God really say... He didn't mean what He said and He didn't say what He meant. In fact, all is as **you** want it to be. Disobey God and be blessed -- you are and you will be as God -- freely determining right and wrong, truth and falsehood (Gn. 3: 3-5, my amplified version)."

As Blessed Catherine Emmerich predicted over a century ago **"everything pertaining to Protestantism gained the upper hand [within Catholicism]." Where this is true** -- in individuals and in existential churches (recall that only two out of seven existential churches in Apoc. 2; 3 were acceptable to God. Are our churches better?) -- **we have the Second Beast or New Age Catholicism.**

New Age Catholicism looks like the LAMB but has the heart and reality of Satan. New Age Catholicism initially pleases MAN -- individually and/or communally.

However, in doing so it abandons the Holy Spirit and **thus** is cursed to be informed by Unholy Spirits. Pleasing MAN soon sours into **dominating MAN** -- according to the "enlightened theories" of ecclesial and secular experts and **authorities**. But, beyond them

171

is **the** Unholy Spirit -- Satan.

THIS IS RUSSIA'S ERRORS AND YET, SOMEHOW, THIS IS ALSO NEW AGE CATHOLICISM WHICH IS (AT LEAST, PART OF) THE SECOND BEAST. SOMEHOW, THE FIRST AND SECOND BEAST ARE ONE -- AT LEAST IN SPIRIT, IF NOT IN FACT -- AS THE THIRTEENTH CHAPTER OF THE APOCALYPSE REVEALS TO US.

Today, in 1991, it seems as if the First Beast has been mortally wounded. However, he will be restored to life by the Second Beast and rule with the Second Beast. **Both Beasts live for/from Man and not God -- thus, they live for/from Satan.**

The Third Revelation of Fatima discloses to us the **fact** that the true faith has been lost within most of the existential churches within Catholicism, Why? It begins: **"Portugal will retain the faith..."** Therefore, it is only logical to presume that the Third Revelation concerns the loss of faith in most (if not, all) of the other nations.

Of greatest importance to us and to the world is the proper papal and episcopal consecration of Russia. Such a consecration will defeat Russia and stop the spread of its **errors.** Russia's (or, the First Beast's) **errors** are **now** flourishing (especially, in the U.S.A.). Russia's **errors** are flourishing within our church and our nation.

Indeed, it is late -- BUT, even now, it is not too late. All we need -- and what we can attain by "enough" lives being consecrated to the Immaculate Heart of Mary -- is **a Pope who will obey God and thus "defy" or "dethrone" MAN.**

The "initial act" of papal obedience will set off a chain reaction which will ultimately result in bringing some or all existential churches along with many people "back into" true FAITH. **Thus,** through that sincere **"Fatima-commanded" reparation** (for its sins), the Church will be graced to begin its desperately needed PURIFICATION AND REFORMATION.

This initial act consists in obeying God's Fatima Command for the proper Ecclesial Consecration of Russia together with a solemnly performed and preached **day of reparation by Pope and bishops.** Those bishops without true faith **won't** obey -- they can be "retired" or excommunicated (and this will help purify the church of "undesirables").

The very act of consecration **includes** an admission by the upper clergy of their sins of disobedience or negligence and a sincere expressed desire to make REPARATION. **Thus,** the Pope and **his** bishops will "naturally" be led to realize, properly repent of and make reparation for their **sins**. Gratefully, they will consecrate Russia and make, as well as preach, a day of reparation -- a day of admitting and repenting of their apparent disobedience to God's Will and to God's Fatima's Commands.

Thus, the Church will be really renewed. **Consequently**, God will bless mankind with a period of peace and spiritual renewal.

[C] A "New Age Compatible" Pope

Unfortunately, Pope John Paul II's speeches and actions in recent years seem to indicate that he is committed to being a major force influencing, within or constituting the Second Beast of the Apocalypse. Unfortunately, in spite of his receiving many special Marian blessings, he shows **no** indication of obeying God's Fatima Command.

Unless God's graces are sufficient to change (and do change) his present direction, perhaps we will have to wait for the next Pope to obey **God's** Fatima Command. Perhaps, **we** who are living right now will have to **experience** the very fullness of the great wrath of God as predicted at Fatima. Perhaps, our progeny will be the recipients of those blessings of true peace which will flow from the Pope's fully obeying God's Fatima Commands.

For the present, let's perceive that which we have become "comfortable with" and, worse yet, "even justify" -- a Pope who, at times, **significantly** speaks and in effect, acts to cooperate with and to support the First Beast. Thus, he is in grave danger of becoming part of the Second Beast.

First of all, we should realize that our blind respect for papal **disobedience** is so strong that we refer to the three **REVELA-TIONS** of Fatima as the three **secrets**.

The third revelation was commanded by God to be revealed **no later than 1960. By the grace of the Spirit of Truth, let us admit the awful and awesome truth -- that Popes disobey God.**

What did our Popes do from 1960 on? They not only disobeyed God, they also managed to pervert Fatima's third REVELATION into Fatima's THIRD SECRET.

This papal disobedience and "cover-up" was followed by the infamous "1984 consecration revisited in 1989" cover-up ("The Fatima Cover-up") -- the cover-up of the **fact** that Russia was **not** consecrated in 1984 as God commanded at Fatima. **At** the very least, Pope John Paul II has gone along with this horrendous "FATIMA COVER-UP."

Pope John Paul II seems to be a victim of pleasing man (especially in the form of the Russian leaders and/or his advisors) and not God. The prestigious **30 DAYS** in an article by the expert, Stefano M. Paci, stated that **the Pope desirous of mentioning Russia in 1984 -- and still not obeying God's Fatima Command (but, at least, showing some willingness to do so by taking a step in the right direction) -- finally and regretfully caved in to his "advisors."** "Bishop Paul Cordes, vice-president of the Council for the Laity, explained: 'It was 1984, and during a private lunch, the Pope spoke of the consecration he had made. He recounted how he had thought, at the outset, to **mention** Russia in the prayer of benediction. But at the suggestion of his advisors, he abandoned the idea. **He could not risk such a direct provocation to the Soviet leaders.** He also told me how much this **renunciation** [of God's will, to please mere men]... had weighed on him (**30 DAYS,** March 1990).'"

Indeed, the Pope should be weighed down by his cowardliness -- by his preferring MAN to God. "Pray for the Pope." Pray that God may overwhelm him with graces to obey GOD and not mere men.

"God will permit the grace of the Consecration of Russia to Mary's Immaculate Heart when a sufficient number are complying with the Message of Fatima" -- Sister Lucy.

In Spite Of Mary's Miracle

How can this Pope who was especially favored by the Virgin be so ungrateful to Her? "Quite fittingly," MEN whom he seems to desire to please tried to **murder** him (the 1981 assassination attempt could have been "an inside job" **AND/OR** it was initiated by the same RUSSIA that the Pope "lovingly" tries not to displease).

Yet, Our Lady preserved him from significant harm. Did he "get the message?" Was he moved to be grateful enough to obey God's Fatima Commands?

Let's recall what happened. Exactly sixty-four years to the day after the first appearance of Our Lady of Fatima (May 13, 1981), Pope John Paul II bent down to pick up a little girl who had a picture of Our Lady of Fatima attached to her sweater. As he did so, two bullets flew over his head. Then, the next two bullets lodged in his body. While recuperating, he claimed that he experienced the October 1917 miracle of Fatima. Unfortunately, not even these great "Marian favors" have been strong enough to convince him to change his present fundamental direction.

Instead, it would seem, he took the vision and God's special providence as a sign to "**speed up**" the process of influencing an emerging One World Government. (He reminds me of Hitler who interpretted the "Fatima-predicted" miraculous light as a favorable sign of success in starting World War II.)

"**Gone was the Pope's presumed time frame involving a leisurely and relatively peaceful evolution...to a veritable new world government (Malachi Martin, THE KEYS OF THIS BLOOD..., p.49).**

"**Now the Pope is in a 'hurried' preparation for that imminent event which will evoke 'an utterly new state of consciousness in all of mankind (p. 456, *ibid*).'**"

Subsequent Fatima Speeches

On May 13, 1982, Pope John Paul II uttered these words at Fatima: "Societies are threatened by apostasy and by moral degradation. The collapse of morality bears with it the collapse of society." Note here the **urgency** of the Pope's message as --continuing to disobey Fatima --he boldly declares at Fatima both Fatima's Message and a veiled prediction of the reason for the (temporary) "collapse" of Russia (in 1989).

Would to God he were graced with Father Maximilian Kolbe's heart: "Modern times are dominated by Satan. The conflict with Hell **cannot** be engaged in by men, even the most clever. **Immaculate Mary alone has from God the promise of victory over Satan.**" Instead, while speaking the truth at Fatima, the Pope failed to obey the truth revealed at Fatima.

After **the sixth Glasnost of Russia's history (the one that began in 1989),** on May 13, 1991, the Pope again spoke at Fatima. He called for "a rebirth of Christian Europe" as he prayed for "an authentic **theology of integral human liberation.**"

The Pope has "all the theology he can handle" in Fatima's Commands. Only the "Fatima theology" will be effective in truly liberating mankind. Yet, even as he speaks at Fatima, the Pope ignores Fatima and its "theology."

In fact, the Pope used the occasion of his visit to Portugal to reiterate his Man-Oriented theology and his opinion that we are joyfully entering "the beginning of a new world ['the post-1989 Glasnost' New Age]". The authentic Fatima Message opposes such Man-Oriented opinions. It presents God-Originating and God-Oriented directions.

Also, before saying Mass on May 13th, the Pope (and, later on, the Bishop of Fatima) met with Sister Lucia. His subsequent speeches made no reference to this meeting. We can be sure that if Sister Lucia had agreed with the Pope's Man-Oriented optimism or with the "party line" that Russia has been properly consecrated, the Pope would have mentioned this.

The Gulf Crisis Of 1991

Perhaps, the Pope's **political** stand during the Gulf Crisis of 1991 also reflects his heart. Does he not believe in MAN and that MEN (the "man-worshipping" experts and authorities) must govern the world as best **they** can (as they twist and/or ignore and/or reject God's will)?

Surprisingly, the Pope came out on the side of Russia (the real instigator of the Gulf War). He sided with Russia and its peace terms although Russia did nothing to stop the madman.

Apparently, before the war, the Pope abandoned the God-given principle that we can and, at times, should KILL unjust aggressors. Hussein tortured and murdered hundreds of thousands of innocent people, yet the Pope took a firm stand against the Gulf War.

The Pope gave the impression to the world that such a war was against the best interests of a New World Order and thus it was "wrong." In effect, he urged the world to side with **Russia** and/or its "Iraqian Puppet."

His **direction** -- the bent of his soul -- seems to be towards MAN and, especially, towards Russia. His outlook seems to be **geopolitical** instead of theological (in the true and unadulterated meaning of "theology").

Effectively, he has **not** changed the direction the church has been taking since Pope Paul VI's reign. Instead, he seems to be **fulfilling** that direction -- especially, on the world scene.

"Paul VI's emphasis on human interest became the basis for discarding sacrifice and prayer and faith and the Sacraments of the Church as the watchwords of hope in this world. They were replaced by **human solidarity,** which became the aim and the centerpiece of Catholic striving. Ecumenism was no longer an attempt to heal the heretical and schismatic rifts that over the centuries had split the one Church Christ had founded on the Rock of Simon Peter's central office. Ecumenism was a means not of genuine healing but of leveling differences of whatever kind between all Christian believers and nonbelievers. That fit nicely with the new central aim of **human solidarity as the hope of mankind.** [taken from THE KEYS OF THIS BLOOD, Malachi Martin]."

This papal emphasis on "human solidarity" now becomes

for Pope John Paul II a compelling obsession to form or "greatly inform" the New World Government. To be sure, he claims devotion to Our Lady, BUT Our Lady's direction opposes the Pope's present direction. (Pray for the Pope!)

The Pope must be graced to truly understand and properly respond to Fatima. The Pope **must** do what God wants in order to remove the demonic within "his own" church -- that's his essential duty.

We consecrate ourselves to Mary so that the Pope may come to realize that he is not here to please MAN, but to please God -- to remove the demonic from within his own sanctuary. To do this, he must obey Fatima's God-given commands and abandon his desires to form or "greatly inform" the New Age and/or the New World Order and/or the FIRST BEAST.

HOW will he accomplish his essential and primary God-given DUTY? HOW will he reform "his" church? By God's special help which can only be attained by obeying the God-given and **proven** prophecy of Fatima.

THE most important Fatima Command he must obey is to consecrate RUSSIA as God commanded at Fatima. **From this act of contrition, repentance, reparation and, above all, OBEDIENCE will flow God's graces for HIS church and thus for the world.**

The Pope should concentrate on "his" Church (1Peter 4:17). However, instead of removing what Sister Lucy of Fatima describes as the "diabolic disorientation" within "his" Church, the Pope at times, seems to foster it (at, least, by his failure to act effectively).

He seems to be preoccupied with "human solidarity," or the New World Order. He even began his pontificate going "in this wrong direction."

"John Paul's own rule of behavior concerning the opening of his Church to 'man in all his works and ambitions to build a secure home on this earth' was the subject of his first encyclical letter, published at Easter 1979 (Malachi Martin, op cit)."

Two recent encyclicals show us that the Pope hasn't changed "his initial direction." Although these encyclicals do not explicitly teach contrary to faith or morals, they do contain or reflect a direction or attitude which is alien to all similar encyclicals which were written before 1960. This direction isn't God's direction as disclosed to us at Fatima.

Two Recent "New Age Compatible" Encyclicals

In 1991, Pope John Paul II issued two encyclicals which (as one distills **the** messages within ambiguity and pious-sounding words) are consonant with his perceiving himself or the church as being "a" or "the" force in the formation and governing of a New World Order.

Pope John Paul II's missionary (?) encyclical, **REDEMPTORIS MISSIO** (Dec., 1990), makes sure that no one is offended. We don't **really** believe that "outside of the Catholic Church there is NO salvation (which is a dogma of the **real** Catholic Church)."

Missionary work becomes optional activity -- except for those who have a **strong** "fraternity-spirit" or "party-spirit." Gone is the absolute urgency of obeying Christ's **COMMAND** to make disciples of all men. (This **urgency** is clearly perceived in **all** encyclicals written about the Church's mission to others, previous to 1960.)

Instead, we have a foundation laid for getting the whole world together -- under one religious system which allows for various religions. The Second Beast of the Apocalypse appeals to every religion which merely claims it is **A** way to God and not **THE** way to God.

No longer are we exposed to a Catholic Church which clearly and dogmatically claims to be **the** way to be saved and which **fervently** and obediently seeks to bring others to the one true fold in order to save them from Hell and in order to avoid being condemned by Christ for **not** doing its God-given duty (for **not really** loving non-Catholics).

<< THE REAL CHURCH TEACHES AS FOLLOWS: -- Many official teachings could be cited. However, I believe that the following **official and binding** CENSURES of Pope Pius IX clearly indicate the true mind of the Real Church and the nature of an increasingly popular false ecumenism.

"Man may in the observance of any religion whatever, find the way of eternal salvation. Anathema sit". **This** is declared to be an **heretical** belief. Taken from (Encyclical **Qui Pluribus**, Nov. 9, 1846)."

"Good hope at least is to be entertained of the eternal salvation of all those who are not at all in the true Church of Christ (the Catholic Church)". Again, **this** belief is censured, not approved. **(Encyclical QUANTO CONFICIAMUR, Aug. 10, 1863)."** >>

Paragraph #10 of **REDEMPTORIS MISSIO** sets the tone for the whole encyclical. "The **universality of salvation** means that it is granted not only to those who explicitly believe in Christ... Salvation... must be made concretely available to all... [how?] salvation in Christ... enlightens them [non-Christians (sic)] in a way which is accommodated to their spiritual and material situation. This grace... **enables each person to attain salvation through his or her free cooperation.**"

Why disturb non-Christians who are endowed with grace which will enable them to attain salvation through their own free co-operation? Why disturb others who are under an "equally valid(?)" system of graces?

[Also, you will notice that it seems to be heretically assumed that Christ's Church is made up of the Christian "Churches." No longer is the Catholic Church explicitly and clearly professed to be **the** Church of Christ and **all other "Christian churches" to be in a state of schism or heresy.**]

Thus, the major missionary encyclical of our day leaves itself open to being perceived as implicitly endorsing a false ecumenism. Following "close on its heels" is the encyclical on governments or world order, **Centesimus Annus** (May, 1991).

Here, the Pope seems to join Russian leaders in bemoaning the failure of classical Communism -- even as he looks forward to the New World Order.

"**Man** is the primary route that the Church must travel in fulfilling her mission (#53)." It seems, in effect, the Pope hopes that the Church (as he sees it) will be a major force in forming (and, perhaps, even becoming) the New World Order which has **MAN** at its very center. After all, **MAN IS THAT PRIMARY ROUTE** (whatever that might mean) **WHICH THE CHURCH MUST TRAVEL IN ORDER TO FULFIL HER MISSION.**

Before we consider "THE REMEDY" for our present situation, it will prove profitable for you to become convinced (or more convinced) that the Catholic Church is an extremely efficient and tightly knit "hierarchical" organization. As the Pope goes, so go "his" bishops.

Therefore, I will present "TWO TYPICAL ROOTS; TWO TYPICAL FRUITS" for your consideration. In this subsequent section, you will see a few concrete examples of how the Pope's apparent or implied direction affects "his" whole church.

Two Typical Roots; Two Typical Fruits

The "real and operative" or existential Catholic Church contains the most efficiently executed "hierarchically-ordered" government in the entire world. Without an army, what the head (the Pope) says, the rest say and DO.

Even in its "present state of decadence", the Catholic Church possesses "miraculous" unity. However, it would seem that God's gift of UNITY -- a unity beyond "natural expectations" -- can be used for evil as well as for good.

As the Pope thinks and acts, the Vatican thinks and acts. As the Pope thinks and acts, the bishops think and act. (Or, could it be that as the Vatican and/or bishops think and act, so does the Pope?)

Redemptoris Missio (12/7/90), Pope John Paul II's encyclical, could possibly give two **impressions** -- **Catholicism** is, in effect, just another **Christian** option ["missionary activity is a matter for all **Christians**" -- #2 (other similar uses of **Christian** could be cited)]; and, any religion is almost just as good as any other decent religion ("the Holy Spirit offers everyone the possibility of sharing in this paschal mystery in a manner known to God" --#10).

This encyclical does not explicitly contain outright error. However, it does employ Rahnerian double-speak. The Catholic dogma ("outside of the Catholic Church, there is no salvation") is no longer clearly and boldly professed. Instead, **"alien impressions"** are conveyed. For example, the Church is optional. Also, for example, **dialogue** is one of the desirable ways we, Cathoics, can attain truth [no longer do we assume what Pope **Saint** Pius X clearly and boldly "presumed" and professed -- that the fullness of truth resides in the Catholic Church (cf., for example, his address in April, 1909 at the beatification of St. Joan of Arc)].

One fruit emanating from this encyclical's **impressions** can be found in a statement issued by two curial congregations (**"Dialogue and Proclamation,"** June 21, 1991). This document contains not only Rahnerian double-speak, but also traces of our American episcopal "I'm sorry; I love you" sentimentalism (as expressed in our national episcopal drafts concerning women).

This curial document assures us that the Holy Spirit will do our real work. We must, however: (1) DIALOGUE -- learn from other religions; (2) "INCULTURATE" -- please the people's expectations and aspirations; (3) APPRECIATE -- not our religion, but the other religions; (4) APOLOGIZE for the radical zeal of past missionary activities; (5) LIVE "RESPECTFULLY" in a pluralistic milieu (for example, don't "rock the boat" by claiming that you have **the truth** and therefore others are wrong). (Of course, these **sentiments** can be found within most of our contemporary religious education programs.)

To be sure, other fruits will emerge out of **Redemptoris Missio** as well as out of other "papal roots" such as that root which was established at **Assisi.**

In October, 1986, **under the leadership of Pope John Paul II,** 150 representatives of various religions met at the sacred Catholic shrine of Assisi. Next to the cross, Buddhist prayer flags placidly drooped.

On the sacred altar, a statue of a Buddha stood above the Tabernacle as Buddha's incense ascended on high. Then, prayers were offered to a Power -- a force or power which reigned over idols, good "God(s)," and demonic powers.

Here, at Assisi, was not the following "ecumenical sentimentalism" practiced (under the direction of the Pope) and thereby implicitly approved? **Whatever MAN decides (e.g. in the area of what or who he, MAN, decides to worship) must be respected.**

Has not this "ecumenical sentimentalism" affected our attitude towards "making converts?" For example, Scot Hahn was "repelled" by two priests when God was leading him away from protestantism into the true Church.

Indeed, the Catholic Church contains an extremely tightly knit upper clergy. As the Pope acts or fails to act -- so do "his" bishops. Therefore, as Sister Lucy often reiterated: PRAY FOR THE POPE. As the Pope goes, so go "his" bishops. As the bishops go, so goes the church.

The Remedy

The Pope and bishops **must** return to the purity and fullness of the true faith. The Church that the Pope is "in charge of" is the one and only true Church of Christ.

As Pope, John Paul II is the "head" of the one true religion from God for man. As Pope, he alone has been chosen by God to be **the** representative before God **of** and **for** mankind. He must "become graced" to "de-focus" on **man** and to "re-focus" on **GOD.**

THUS, will he begin to be further graced by God to do his "job" properly.

By God's grace -- which will be attained as a sufficient number of us live **consecrated to the Immaculate Heart of Mary** -- the

Pope will be led to obey the Fatima Command concerning the consecration of Russia. THUS, will "his" Church become what it should be and CONSEQUENTLY the world will attain a period of peace.

The Pope's GREAT TEST of obedience and humility consists in admitting "his errors" and those of "his" Church; and, therefore, calling for a special **day of reparation**; and, of consecrating Russia to the Immaculate Heart of Mary ("collegially," etc.) as God commanded at Fatima. From **that** act of obedience will flow God's blessings on the one true Church and **thus** on mankind -- "a period of peace will be given mankind."

Will the Second Beast or a "forerunner" of the Second Beast materialize before a Pope obeys Fatima's **God-given command?** I personally contend that such will be our end-times scenario.

Personally, I fail to see how the present Pope [who maintains the secrecy of the Third Revelation of Fatima against God's will that it be made known; and, who apparently "covers-up" his apparent disobedience to God's Fatima Commands (to make and preach with all of "his" bishops a day of REPARATION and to properly consecrate Russia); and, who seems to be impelled by a conviction that _he_ will be a major human factor in the formation of the New Age] will ever cooperate with God's graces, acknowledge his disobedience, repent; and, finally, obey God's Fatima Commands.

However, we should not pronounce any type of final judgment on the Pope's apparent disobedience. Nor does his apparent disobedience justify our **real** disobedience. **In fact, according to Our Lady of Fatima, OUR failure to live the Fatima Commands is responsible for the Pope not attaining sufficiently overwhelming graces to obey God's Fatima Commands.**

"God will permit the grace of the Consecration of Russia to Mary's Immaculate Heart when a sufficient number are complying with the Message of Fatima" -- Sister Lucy.

Each of us should explicitly consecrate himself to the Immaculate Heart of Mary and live this consecration. Each of us should join the real Sister Lucy and "pray for the Pope" as well as for the many clerics whom she described as "blind leaders of the blind." Lastly, each of us should do what he can to spread the God-given Fatima Message and urge our bishops and Pope to obey the God-given Fatima commands.

From their "sacramental act" (of making and preaching REPARATION; and, of consecrating RUSSIA as God commands) will flow the much needed reformation of Christ's one and only true Church. As peace, unity and proper government return to Christ's Church, the whole world will share in God's blessings and a period of peace will be given to mankind.

"In the end, My Immaculate Heart will triumph. The Holy Father will consecrate Russia to me. It will be converted and a period of peace will be granted to the world" -- Our Lady of Fatima.

Final victory is assured. It all depends on the Pope. Yet, our prayers and labors will determine how soon God will bless us and which Pope will be sufficiently graced to obey God's Fatima Commands.

In any event, Mary's Remnant will be saved.

Select Bibliographical List

Father Nicholas Gruner S.T.L.; S.T.D. (Cand.)
World Enslavement or Peace . . . It's Up To The Pope,
Immaculate Heart Publications, 1988, 640 pages.

Father Joseph de St. Marie O.C.D.
Theological Reflections, on the act of Consecration of the World by
Pope John Paul II in Fatima. Marianum Ephemerides Mariologiae.
Rome, 1982, 54 pages. It is also printed in English, 1983, 36 pages.

Frère Michel de la Sainte Trinité
The Whole Truth About Fatima
Vol . I   Science and The Facts, 1989, 549 pages.
Vol. II   The Secret and The Church, 1989, 850 pages.
Vol. III   The Third Secret, 1990, 874 pages.
Immaculate Heart Publications.

Sister Lucy of Fatima
Fatima In Lucia's Own Words, Ravengate, 1976, 200 pages.

Francis Johnson
Fatima - The Great Sign, Tan, 1980, 148 pages.

Deidre Manifold
Fatima and The Great Conspiracy, Militia of Our Immaculate
Mother, 1987, 144 pages.

William Thomas Walsh
Our Lady of Fatima, Doubleday, 1954, 223 pages.

> ## All the above books are available through the publisher of this book.

The Awesome Fatima Consecrations
Order Form

Dear Father Trinchard,

I want to help spread the authentic Fatima Message. Please send me _____ copies of *The Awesome Fatima Consecrations*.

Enclosed is my payment in the amount of $ _____.

(Please print your name and address in easily legible BLOCK letters)

NAME _____

ADDRESS_____

CITY, STATE _____

ZIP/POSTAL CODE _____

************* **CUT AND MAIL ABOVE** *************

Quantity Prices (U.S. Funds)
(Order In Bulk And Save)

No. of Books Ordered	Total Book Cost	Postage and Handling	TOTAL COST
1	$9.95	$1.00	$10.95
3	$28.00	$2.00	$30.00
5	$44.00	$3.00	$47.00

OVER 5 -- $9.00 per book (including p.&h.)

Postage costs are based on shipment to one address only.
Please include cheque or money order payable in U.S. Funds.

ORDER FROM: **META**
P.O. Box 6012
Metairie, LA.
70009-6012

I

Other Books Available By
Father Paul Trinchard

APOSTASY WITHIN --- (Foreward by Father Malachi Martin. A popular analysis of the present condition of the Catholic Church in America with suggestions for effective action).
$14.95 U.S. per book plus $1.25 p.&h.
{this book is in it's second printing}

GOD'S WORD --- (Foreward by Father Vincent Miceli. An "easy-reading" refutation of modern liberal Catholic Biblical scholarship; and, reading this book will help restore your faith in the Bible as being the Word of God).
$12.95 U.S. per book plus $1.25 p. & h.

SPECIAL: Both books for $25.00 plus $2.00 p. & h.

(These Special Prices Can Only Be Obtained From Meta)

**************** CUT OUT AND MAIL ****************

(Please print your name and address in easily legible BLOCK letters)

NAME _____

ADDRESS _____

CITY, STATE _____

ZIP/POSTAL CODE _____

Quantity		Total
	Apostasy Within	$
	God's Word	$
	Special Set of Both Books	$
	Sub-Total	$
	Plus Postage and Handling	$
	Total Enclosed U.S. Funds	$

Please Enclose Check Or Money Order In U.S. Funds

Send Order To: META
P.O. Box 6012
Metairie, LA.
70009 - 6012